MUSHROOM

A Complete Mushroom Cultivation Guide on How to Grow
Gourmet Mushrooms and Identify Wild Common
Mushrooms and Other Fungi for Beginners

By Tom Gordon

© **Copyright 2019 - All rights reserved.**

The content contained within this book may not be reproduced, duplicated or transmitted without direct written permission from the author or the publisher.

Under no circumstances will any blame or legal responsibility be held against the publisher, or author, for any damages, reparation, or monetary loss due to the information contained within this book. Either directly or indirectly.

Legal Notice:

This book is copyright protected. This book is only for personal use. You cannot amend, distribute, sell, use, quote or paraphrase any part, or the content within this book, without the consent of the author or publisher.

Disclaimer Notice:

Please note the information contained within this document is for educational and entertainment purposes only. All effort has been executed to present accurate, up to date, and reliable, complete information. No warranties of any kind are declared or implied. Readers acknowledge that the author is not engaging in the rendering of legal, financial, medical or professional advice. The content within this book has been derived from various sources. Please consult a licensed professional before attempting any techniques outlined in this book.

By reading this document, the reader agrees that under no circumstances is the author responsible for any losses, direct or indirect, which are incurred as a result of the use of information contained within this document, including, but not limited to, — errors, omissions, or inaccuracies.

Table of Contents

Mushrooms 1

Introduction 2

Chapter 1 - The Story Of The Mushroom 6

Chapter 2 - Why Choose Mushrooms? 24

Chapter 3 - Mushroom Basics 41

Chapter 4 - Growing Mushrooms...52

Chapter 5 - Ways To Use Mushrooms..77

Chapter 6 - Foraging And Identification......................................94

Chapter 7- The Power Of A Medicinal Mushroom 98

Chapter 8- Common Mistakes To Avoid When Growing Mushrooms 117

Bonus Chapter - Growing Gourmet Mushrooms For Profit – Faq...123

Conclusion 128

Mushroom Facts..132

Mushroom Cultivation 133

Introduction 134

Chapter 1 - Best Of Mushrooms...136

Chapter 2 - Overview Of Mushroom Cultivation 147

Chapter 3 - Choosing Your Mushrooms 155

Chapter 4 - Setting Up A Grow Room 175

Chapter 5 - Growing Methods 200

Chapter 6 - Getting Started With The Growing Process............222

Chapter 7 - Preserving Mushrooms..234

Chapter 8 - Understanding Fungi 259

Chapter 9 - Profiting From Gourmet Mushrooms.....................271

Chapter 10 - Delicious Recipes For Mushroom Lovers 279

Final Words...284

MUSHROOMS
A Beginner's Guide to Cultivating and Using Mushrooms

By Tom Gordon

INTRODUCTION

Welcome to the world of mushrooms! This book will provide everything you need to be a prepared steward of cultivating and using mushrooms to the necessity of your own uses. We will cover everything from the health benefits of mushrooms to how to grow them, from the history of mushrooms to the way they are used in modern-day religious ceremonies.

Each of section of the book can be read independently of each other, so feel free to skip around to the information that is most necessary for you.

As a quick summary to help you get started, in Chapter One we'll discover the importance of using mushrooms to grow and cultivate for your own personal usage. We will discuss the health benefits of mushrooms, how to use mushrooms with care and how to make sure you are handling mushrooms that are not poisonous.

In chapter 2, we will quickly walk through the parts of a mushroom and the life cycle of the mushroom for you to have the most preparation possible for when you decide to grow mushrooms for yourself. It is important to have all the jargon down as you become an experienced mushroom farmer so that when you run into problems (believe me, you'll run into plenty), you will be able to handle them by yourself and research using proper terms when necessary. We will also discuss what a mushroom is.

Next, in chapter 3, we'll talk about the most popular mushrooms to grow for yourself, including varieties such as Crimini, Maitake, Portobello, Shiitake, White Button, and Oyster. We will talk through the health benefits of each one, the difficulty in growing each, and what materials you need to start growing them.

We will go into the specifics of growing mushrooms, covering subjects such as soiling, watering, fertilizing, pruning, harvesting, and other topics related to these. This will be heavy on the technical talk, so be sure to read chapter 2 before you read this chapter.

In Chapter 4, we walk through how to use mushrooms most effectively, whether that be in the kitchen, for medicine, added health benefits, religious ceremonies, and more. Lastly, chapter 6 will be where we will talk through the mistakes to avoid while working with mushrooms and other important notes.

In Chapter 5, we look briefly at foraging for mushrooms and how to identify them, along with a list of questions you need to ask yourself about every mushroom you find – that way, you have a good idea of whether they are safe to eat or not.

In Chapter 6, we will dive in-depth into medicinal mushrooms, discussing what they are, and the physiological effects of the mushrooms. Then we look into the impact on individual systems in the human body, such as the endocrine system, the cardiovascular system, and so on. We'll end the chapter by looking at five specific mushrooms and how they can boost your health.

In Chapter 7, we will discuss some of the more common problems you might encounter when cultivating mushrooms, such as not fruiting, spoiling after harvest, and more.

And, as a bonus chapter, I will answer 12 of the most commonly asked questions about growing gourmet mushrooms for profit.

Growing mushrooms is an amazing journey. I hope you enjoy it.

MUSHROOMS

CHAPTER 1

THE STORY OF THE MUSHROOM

No example of the mushroom's impact on the world around us is quite like the fungi that killed an emperor, which changed the face of Europe entirely. Charles VI was the Holy Roman Emperor in Vienna, Austria, from the 1st of October 1685 and died on the 20th of October 1740. On the 10th of October, at the age of 55, he was fighting a nasty cold as he was struggling under ruling a harsh political campaign in a time of possible bankruptcy, as this was nature's way of telling him to take some time to rest instead of pushing himself. An old saying was that to beat a cold, he must eat to regain his strength; he decided to have a bit of his favorite meal - mushrooms stewed in Catalan oil. Somehow the deadly *Amanita phalloides*, also known as the Death Cap Mushroom, ended up in his stew. He survived for ten days but succumbed to his illness eventually.

After his untimely death, Marie Theresa, Archduchess of Austria, had to bear arms to defend her inheritance from the forces of Poland, Saxony, Spain, Prussia, Bavaria, and France. This was known as the Austrian Succession War from 1740 to 1748, and while Maria was able to save her crown, there was still a huge change in Europe. According to some scholars, the instability in Austria seemed to even leak into the War of Jenkin's Ear between the British, Spanish, and the Caribbean, and affected people as far as India; this event affected the Revolutionary War in the Americas. As Voltaire once said: "A dish of mushrooms changed the destiny of Europe."

In the history of food groups, nothing has been so loved and hated at the same time than that of the mushroom. The terms "mycophilia" and "mycophobia" are widely used now to describe these two broad camps of people. Many eastern countries have historically loved the mushroom for its seemingly magical abilities to treat patients from everything from anxiety to cancer, from headaches to gout. At the same time, in western countries, the authors have gone so far as to call the mushroom "the devil's food" by the Roman emperor Nero, or as the philosopher Denis Diderot said about them: "[Mushrooms] are not really good but to be sent back to the dung heap where they are born". No other food group has been called such terrible names, while at the same time being called the "food of the Gods."

The truth of it all is that the mushroom is a healthy and life-bringing organism that is an important part of any diet as well as incredibly necessary in the completion of the carbon and phosphorus cycle. They are nature's number #1 composting agents, and without them, there would be miles and miles of buildups of dead trees in Northern Oregon and elephant dung piles for kilometers in India.

They are full of nutrients and health benefits for all sorts of patients, such as reduction of anxiety for mentally-ill patients to having a wonderful number of antioxidants for a healthy immune system. If you don't end up growing mushrooms for yourself, at least do it for your loved ones around you that can benefit from these wonderful fungi.

Over the years, humans have moved from thinking of mushrooms in terms of good and bad and to a way of thinking that is more based on scientific research and inquiry. We have moved on from superstition and old wives' tales and into medical research and culinary ingenuity for the benefit of people's health as well as their taste buds. This does not mean, however, that they are not still used widely in religious and spiritual purposes, specifically in countries such as Tanzania and Mongolia. Mushrooms need to be treated with respect, for in them carry both life and death.

Louis Pasteur: A Quick Bio

Louis Pasteur was never a big drinker himself, but his scientific duties required him to solve problems with French brewing techniques, a skill that has been "brewing" for thousands of years. In 1857, he began his research on yeast under a microscope only to discover that yeast was a living organism. As he started to do experiments on these newfound organisms, he found that the absence of free oxygen caused the yeast to obtain its energy by decomposing substances that contained oxygen. This process is now known as anaerobic respiration or fermentation, which is the breaking down of sugars in grains and converting them into alcohol, CO2, and other beer flavors.

He also found that to keep beer longer, it would need to be heated at a certain temperature for a short period. This is a process we now call pasteurization, which is now used in everything from wines to cheeses, canned foods to syrup.

Benefits

You are thinking of growing your own mushrooms, and I believe that you do not need to be told that it is a good idea, because you obviously already know that. What you want to know is why it is good to do so. Depending on individual studies and their results, mushrooms are, overall, the superheroes of the fungi kingdom. Mushrooms have been shown to inhibit the growth of cancer cells, to help improve the immune system and reduce blood glucose levels in cancer patients, and prolong the lives of different types of patients and kill certain viruses. Mushrooms are also found to be a wonderful resource for potassium, protein, copper, riboflavin, pantothenate, vitamin D, and selenium. They are especially a great source of protein.

For those of you who are attempting to live a vegetarian lifestyle, or at least stay away from meat on certain days, mushrooms have been a meat substitute for hundreds of years because of their high protein content; they are 10-45 percent protein when dried (they are 80% water on average) When monks were going on meat fasts, or when farmstock was at a low amount, people would use mushrooms as a viable substitute for fleshy proteins. Mushrooms are also extremely important as a medicine, as we will talk about more in chapter 4. They are known to be taken as a whole, created into powders, herbal mixtures, teas, and concentrates.

Research by Paul Stamets has led many to switch their belief system to a more positive one when it comes to mushrooms. Paul Stamets and Battelle Laboratories joined up at Bellingham Washington to conduct a series of experiments. They had four piles of dirt that were saturated with diesel and other petroleum waste. They had a control pile, one was treated with enzymes, another was treated with bacteria, and the last one was treated with mushroom mycelium. The mycelium became saturated with the oil and converted the pile into oyster mushrooms. But that's not all. The mushrooms let out spawns of spores, and then that attracted insects, and then that attracted birds that brought seeds, and that completely changed the environment. It became an oasis of vegetation. The PAHs, or Polycyclic Aromatic Hydrocarbons, went from 10,000 PPM to 200 PPM in eight weeks, an astounding figure, to say the least. The mushroom is a gateway into more productive environments and the nurse for hurting ones.

Paul Stamets has also done research on Agarikon Mushrooms, which are found in the old-grown forest, first described by Dioscorides in the 1st century as a treatment against consumption. It grows in the Northwest of the United States and is extremely rare. They were found to be extremely helpful towards poxviruses. The U.S. Defense Department states that any compound with a selectivity index of two or more is considered active, while ten or more is considered to be very active.

After this worked so well against the smallpox viruses, they went for the flu virus. After tests with individual mushrooms, they switched to trying blended concentrations. This allowed them to take the good from all of the mushrooms they had available to see what the new selectivity index would be. They had a selectivity index of 1,000, which is ridiculously high, almost unheard of in this field. This is all to say that mushrooms are amazingly good for you, and choosing to grow them is an extremely good idea.

Mushrooms are also extremely easy to grow. Once small mushrooms called primordia start to pop up in your growing container after a few weeks, it should take less than five days before you have full-grown mushrooms ready to harvest and eat. You will be spending a small amount of money on the substrate as well as the spawn needed to grow them properly, and because mushrooms do not have chloroplasts and are therefore not plants, you do not need to buy a fancy grow light to have them flourish. All they truly need is room temperature and humidity, so spraying them with a bit of water every day will help them grow wonderfully.

General Knowledge of Mushrooms

In this section, we will go through a couple of different sections of information that have to do with mushrooms. This will give you a general overview of different types of mushrooms, the different categories of mushrooms, their characteristics, and more. Refer to this section when you have a quick question about mushrooms and fungi in general. Here is a table of contents for you to find what you need faster:

Zombie Ant Fungus: What is it?

The proper name for this fungus is Ophiocordyceps unilateralis. Alfred Russel Wallace first discovered this pathogenic insect fungus in 1859, and it was most commonly found in tropical rainforest ecosystems. It affects a certain tribe of ants, and it is characterized by the alteration of specific behavior patterns of the ant that is infected, causing the infected hosts to leave their colony and go on the forest floor where the best suitable environment and temperature is for fungal growth to occur. The ant then crawls to a low-hanging leaf and attaches itself to the underside of the leaf where it eventually dies, and the fruit body of the fungus starts to grow out of the skull of the ant. This whole process takes about a week to occur, including the stage where the fungus erupts from the ant's head, and it releases spores to reproduce and infect more ants. This whole process is so devastating to ant colonies that ant drones have been known to carry away infected ants away from the colony in order to not be exposed to fungal spores.

What are different mushroom habitats?

Most fungi are found in very specific places around the world, in specific environments, so naturally, it is important to be able to recognize these main habitats to best identify and find mushrooms to your liking. And while this book is mainly about cultivating and growing your own mushrooms, it follows that it is important to know more about mushrooms in foraging/ identification of mushrooms as well to develop a love for mushrooms overall. They are mostly found in woodlands and grasslands, and for the scope of this book, we will focus on common areas, mostly within the United States.

WOODLAND

Many varieties of woodland support different types of fungal life. Many mushrooms prefer acidic peaty soil, with beech or birch trees, as well as pine trees. Mossy pine forests are rich in fungi as well as oak woodlands, so much so that some fungi are found to be growing on chestnuts as well.

GRASSLAND

Although there are many types of grassland, from wheat and barley fields to more industrialized fertilized grasslands, mushrooms are to be found in all of them. The mushrooms in these habitats are directly associated with the grass and droppings of animals that graze there. There are fertilized pastures and unfertilized meadows, in which fertilized pastures are typically grazed on by farm animals, so many mushrooms grow on the dung of farm animals. Unfertilized meadows have many plant and mushroom species that have to compete with other mushrooms to survive in low-nutrient areas.

How do I tell if a mushroom is edible, inedible, or poisonous?

Most poisonous mushrooms look similar to edible ones, so all cultivators and foragers are strongly advised to make sure they are familiar with poisonous types of mushrooms and to be at least able to identify characteristics of poisonous mushrooms. Popular modes of identifying mushrooms include staining tests, observing the texture of the mushroom, smelling the mushroom for any distinctive smells, perhaps tasting a small portion of the mushroom and spitting out quickly after (this is only if you are sure it is not poisonous, and rather have to decide on whether the mushroom is edible or not), and trying out various chemical tests on the mushroom. The best thing is to get yourself a good identification booklet and use it when you gather samples from the field to be **ABSOLUTELY** certain that what you are consuming is an edible mushroom that will not kill you instantly. Have fun!

How to Pick a Mushroom

Most species can be harvested with a knife, shears, or a small saw that can be very helpful for the hardier samples. Do your best to keep the fungi in a closed container so that it does not dry out and so that it is not exposed to oxygen too early in the process of identification. When foraging for mushrooms, here is a shortlist of materials you should bring with you:

1. Flat Basket
2. Knife
3. Tweezers
4. Collection Box
5. Hand Lens
6. Camera with Macro Lens
7. Notepad and Pencils

Most Common Edible North American Mushrooms

The Field Mushroom - This very common mushroom can be found in lawns after a light rainfall and is a close relative to the common white button and portobello mushroom found in stores around the world. It can be found in fields of grass, and its preferred substrate is the ground. It can be seen in the early fall.

Caesar Mushroom - This mushroom mostly grows in hardwood forests with a ground substrate. This mushroom is quite a beautiful sample, being that the cap is a bright red/red-orange variety with a yellow stem. Its spore color is white, and it has an orange-yellow gill color.

Honey Mushroom - This mushroom is unique in that it grows on wood, even sometimes buried wood. It prefers hardwood and conifer forests as well as stumps in residential lawns. It has a clustered growth habit, meaning that it grows together uniquely, originating from one central point. The best way to identify this mushroom is to look for the ring on the stem.

Wood Ears - Also known as a Jew's Ear, this is a wonderful edible found growing on wood in hardwood and conifer trees. This is a jelly mushroom and has a pinkish-brown color to it, a very easy one to identify with no poisonous look-alikes.

Giant Puffballs - There are no look-alikes to the *Calvatia Gifantea*, a fairly unique mushroom, to say the least. They are pure white and are about the size of a basketball or smaller. When eaten, they sort of taste like plain ice cream. They grow on the ground almost anywhere in the US, but specifically in the Midwest.

Common Chanterelle - These mushrooms have a beautiful yellow color to them, like fresh paint on the side of a house. They have false gills not used for the disposal of spores. They prefer to grow on the ground of hardwood forests, specifically under oaks.

Smooth Chanterelle - As opposed to Common Chanterelles, these mushrooms have smooth gills that are not as sharp. These grow in abundance in the fall in North America and are easy to find because of their bright orange-yellow color. Like Common Chanterelles, these grow on the ground in hardwood forests under oaks.

Black Trumpets - This mushroom is found growing on the forest floor near oaks, and most of the time, there is moss nearby. There are no lookalikes to this unique mushroom, being that it is all black, vase-shaped, and it has very thin flesh. These are known as very good edibles, whether it is eaten fresh or dried out. It is also known as the Horn of Plenty.

Brick Tops - These mushrooms are mainly found on the wood of hardwood forests with a gill color of white, gray, and purple varieties. There are not many lookalikes out there, so no problems there. They grow in clusters on hardwood stumps — a very tasty and hardy variety.

Lobster Mushrooms - These mushrooms are actually a sort of parasite on a *Russula* or *Lactarius* species and is usually found in forests. This mushroom is easy to spot by its bright orange-red color, and it also gets its name from its color — a very interesting and edible mushroom.

Pear-Shaped Puffball - This is a smaller variety of puffball that grows on downed trees in a hardwood forest. It is a beautiful variety with its brownish-white skin, a relative of the Giant Puffball we discussed earlier. They usually grow in clusters and are fairly abundant in areas that they are found. These are one of my personal favorites to eat, tasting similar to Giant Puffballs.

The Parasol - This mushroom is found in conifer and hardwood forests alike on the ground with white spores and gills. This is a famous mushroom for certain foragers because of the hearty taste and abundance of the mushroom. This mushroom has brown scales and a double-edged ring on the stem that will sometimes move up and down.

Oysters - These are one of the most common mushrooms out there, and they usually grow on wood in hardwood forests. They have a white color and can be found year-round in the United States. The best way to identify this mushroom is by paying attention to the fact that they grow off the side of the wood in a shelf-style. This mushroom is very easy to cultivate as well. They also have very widely spaced gills, an important factor in identifying them.

Deer Mushroom - Similar to the Oyster mushroom, this mushroom likes to grow on rotten wood. They also appear in the spring, as oyster mushrooms do as well. However, as oyster mushrooms grow in clusters, deer mushrooms grow by themselves. Also, the stem of the mushroom is centered, as the oyster mushroom is not. This mushroom has a very earthy mushroom and soggy when cooked.

Cauliflower Mushrooms - This one's name is an obvious one; it looks like a head of cauliflower. It is mostly white and grows on the ground of hardwood forests around the United States. Anything that looks similar to this one is also a good edible, specifically its brother *Sparassis crispa*.

Morel - This mushroom is well sought out for in the wild because it is not able to be cultivated, a very tasty one at that.

Chicken of The Woods - This mushroom has an interesting color as well as an interesting name. It is a good edible with a very bright orange color, a good example of a non-poisonous colorful mushroom. This is a polypore mushroom in that it does not have gills, but it, in fact, has pores to release its spores. This is one of my personal favorite mushrooms.

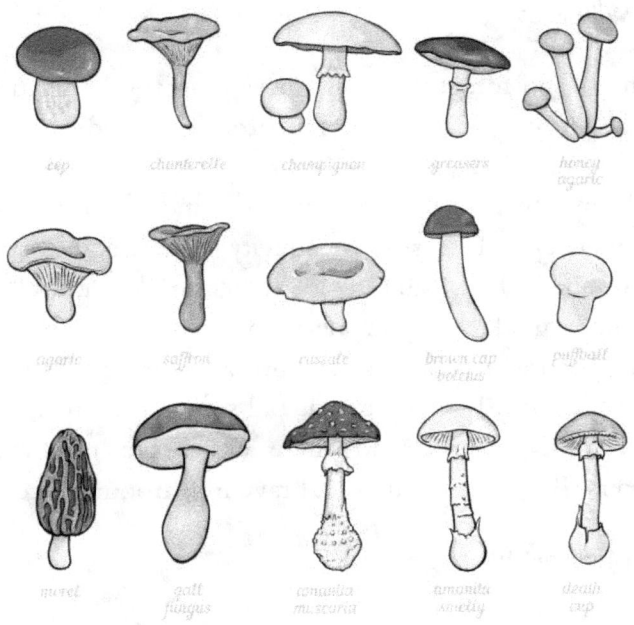

Seven Categories of Mushrooms, And Other Information

1. Cultivated Mushrooms

These mushrooms are the ones that are cultivated and grown commercially. Most farmers can use a very cheap way to work on growing mushrooms. We will talk in more depth about this later. You are able to turn wild mushrooms into cultivated mushrooms by the process of propagation, which we will talk about later as well. Always be ready to identify the mushrooms that are grown by other farmers as well, just as a useful second opinion.

2. Wild Mushrooms

Hunters and foragers harvest these mushrooms from the world around them. Wild mushrooms include truffles, morels, and chanterelles. These can only be grown in the wild, and there is no way at this time to grow them commercially. This sort of activity is where it is most important in being able to identify mushrooms well, so consult a guide or someone who knows what they are doing before you eat that mushroom that you found in your backyard. Remember this old saying: "There are old mushroom hunters, and there are brave mushroom hunters. But there are no old, brave mushroom hunters."

3. Medical Mushrooms

These are mushrooms used strictly for medical purposes. This may include anything from simple health benefits like getting enough vitamins in your diet, or it could be as serious as treating Alzheimer's disease and destroying cancer cells. It seems to me that these mushrooms are the most important ones to focus on when thinking about how to grow mushrooms, and with these types of mushrooms, there are the most amount of uses for them. Some fungi have also been known to reduce cholesterol and been used as antibacterial agents. This includes reishi, turkey tail, and Chaga mushrooms.

4. Psychoactive Mushrooms

We will not be focusing too much attention on these mushrooms in the scope of this book, but when used for research and overall health benefits, these mushrooms are extremely helpful for humans and animals alike. Psychoactive mushrooms, which have the ingredient psilocybin in them, have been used to treat Alzheimer's disease, as well as mitigate the effects of depression and anxiety in certain patients. They are extremely helpful when used in inappropriate ways and can be extremely unhelpful and harmful when used in inappropriate ways.

5. **Edible Mushrooms**

These are obviously mushrooms that are edible and ready to be eaten by human beings. They are used in different diets to obtain specific results desired by the one consuming them, specifically for vitamins and minerals, calories, and macros such as carbs, fats, and proteins.

6. **Poisonous Mushrooms**

These are obviously poisonous species of mushrooms found in the wild that are not supposed to be eating, and this helps clarify why it is so important to identify mushrooms in the wild positively. Many poisonous species look very similar to edible mushrooms at different parts of their development, so research and buying your own field guide are very important when becoming interested in foraging for your own food in general. The effects of poisonous mushrooms can range from making you very ill, causing damage to your liver, headaches, or even death in some cases. Be careful out there.

7. **Useful Mushrooms (For Other Reasons)**

These mushrooms are like edible mushrooms and medical mushrooms, but they are used for different purposes by a variety of cultures around the world. They are not meant to be eaten but rather used for other reasons. Most famously, mushrooms can be used for something called bioremediation, which is the act of cleaning up the environment. They are readily available to break down oil and other contaminants and use the vitamins inside of the mushrooms to create even better compost out of the materials. Scientists are always researching how the mushrooms can be used to replace fossil fuels, packaging materials, cleaning products, and even textiles. By the way, the research is going; mushrooms can be used for a huge amount of different reasons in the near future.

There are four major groups of genera of fungi: Gasteroids, Polypore, Boletes, and Agarics.

- Gasteroids are the ball fungi such as the common puffball

- Polypores are your shelf fungi that dwell in trees with no stipe

- Boletes are your short and stumpy ground-dwelling gilled mushrooms

- Agarics look most like your typical mushroom that houses the death cap mushroom.

MUSHROOMS

Agaric Honey Mushroom

CHAPTER 2

WHY CHOOSE MUSHROOMS?

There are many reasons to grow mushrooms. They are better for the environment, they help you have a deeper appreciation of nature, you will save money at the grocery store, it's an overall wonderful activity, and strangely enough, growing mushrooms will make you into an even better person than you are now!

Mushrooms also have health benefits, such as improved heart health, protection against diabetes, Alzheimer's and dementia, cancer, and they can even help with pregnancy.

Why Grow Mushrooms?

To grow a mushroom is to take part in history itself, as we have explored earlier. Think of the importance that mushrooms have played in the history of the world, and how they have changed the face of Europe in the case of Charles VI, and the ideas of countless authors and writers, poets and storytellers over the years. The history of the mushroom is enough to make this an interesting addition to your home garden and a talking piece for the neighbors when they see your growing parcels, while your frantically explain the actual usage of the mushrooms is less psychedelic than otherwise believed. (As an added note, the focus of this book will be on the legal cultivation of mushrooms that are used by law-abiding citizens, as opposed to their other uses that the author of this book does not necessarily agree with.) But don't sell mushrooms short, because they have more benefits to them then you are most likely aware of.

There are many reasons to grow mushrooms. They are better for the environment, they help you have a deeper appreciation of nature, you will save money at the grocery store, it's an overall wonderful activity, and strangely enough, growing mushrooms will make you into an even better person than you are now! These five reasons all have a few more reasons for growing them within the reasons themselves, so there are upwards of about twenty reasons why you should be growing mushrooms, which is a ton more than I bet you thought about when you started reading this book. We will go through these five reasons in this chapter, and throughout reading this book, you will subtly see more and more reasons pop up all over the pages of this book, like mushrooms tend to do in meadow overnight.

It is better for the environment.

As Paul Stamets advocates in his TedTalk (see references), mushrooms could be a huge part of saving the environment from destruction because of human-based affairs. Mushrooms are amazing because they can create food from waste, so they are self-sufficient, they can be used as animal feed, they help build soil, and they are useful in supporting the growth of other crops and get rid of the need of fertilizer. Check out these reasons to help yourself become an even better steward for the environment.

Create Food from Waste

As we learned, mushrooms are some of the best recyclers in nature, and they can break up almost any carbon-based materials that are produced on farms or by small families. Whether you own a farm or are simply a person from the city looking to reduce their ecological footprint, you can use the materials you normally throw away, such as corn cobs, coffee beans, peanut shells, and many other materials to grow mushrooms upon. Imagine a crop that is produced on the waste of other crops. Amazing!

Self Sufficient

There is a sense of pride that comes from producing your own food. It's a feeling that is long lost from a world of delivery food and instant gratification. You will be able to create as many mushrooms as you wish to fit your own personal needs that you have throughout the years. You won't have to rely on anyone else but yourself on how often you get your mushrooms, but instead, you can be the boss of your own future. Later on, in this book, we will discuss how you can make this a reality.

Animal Feed

If you are a farmer, you also probably have some livestock around that require some food to stay in the best shape possible. When mushrooms are first harvested, they are full of protein and many important vitamins that they absorbed from the waste they grew upon. Studies have shown that livestock of all types benefit from eating mushrooms, and have resulted in improvements in health, digestion, and their immune system. Mushrooms are basically a renewable resource that is extremely healthy for you and your animals.

Building Soil

Also known as "spent spawn," most mushroom growers don't use them for much, so it is very easy to get these leftovers for free. These homemade compost piles are full of benefits, such as their amount of nutrients as well as increased water-holding ability. Mushrooms also help produce actual soil as a byproduct of their growing cycle. This is an amazing trait for an organism that can be eaten as well, a truly renewable resource that more people should know about. These fungi are perfect for corporate and casual farmers alike.

Supporting Crops

Certain fungi can improve the health of many different crops, as proven through empirical evidence. Fungi can make phosphorous usable through the digestion of organic matter. This nutrient is not usually used by plants, as the phosphorus cycle usually deals with rocks and clays, so this means many farmers can use less fertilizer and produce an equal amount of food for their effort. This is very helpful and healthy for both the farmer and the crops themselves. Growing mushrooms alongside your other crops could be very healthy for both.

It Helps You Create a Greater Appreciation for Nature

As you start to grow any sort of crop, you will start to appreciate how they grow in their usual environment. This is especially true for mushrooms because of the rapid growth they have once they start to sprout up. Seeing mushrooms in their natural setting with make you stop with awe and see nature how it was meant to be observed just a bit more. As we touch on next, mushrooms are some of the most beautiful and abundant species on the planet, so they are for sure able to give you a greater appreciation for nature itself.

Mushrooms are Beautiful Organisms

Mushrooms are some of the most widely diverse organisms on the planet, and because there are so many species that you can grow on your own, you will never tire of observing these wonderful specimens. Try out several different mushrooms to get the full effect, and try growing them around the house in interesting ways to add some awesome effects and talking points. If you don't believe me, check out this https://www.boredpanda.com/mushroom-photography full of beautiful mushrooms. In your spare time, check out puffballs, *Mycena Chlorphos, Marasmius Haematocephalus,*

Rhodotus Palamatus, and *Phallus Indusiatus.* One of these actually glows in the dark. George Weller once wrote to his wife: "Darling, I am writing this to you by the light of five mushrooms."

The Growing Cycle is Beautiful

Mushrooms are unique in that they grow off of the waste of other plants and animals, and the way they do this is even more unique. Once you see your first pile covered in mycelium, you will know what I mean, as it covers it slowly over time with its long, white branches extending over the substrate. You will then start to see Small mushrooms called primordia pop up all around the substrate you have laid down, and within a few days after that, you will have fully grown mushrooms seemingly coming out of thin air. It truly makes sense why people used to think that fairies and lightning storms brought about these unique organisms.

You will Save Grocery Money

If you start growing your own supply of mushrooms, you will never have to go shopping for them again. The supplies needed to grow your own mushrooms are minimal, and the effort it takes is also very small, so deciding to grow your own mushrooms is a wonderful choice economically, and homegrown mushrooms actually taste better than store-bought ones anyways oh, so it's a win-win.

They Taste Better than Store-Bought Mushrooms

Mushrooms growing at your home do not have to travel there; they do not need to be packaged, and they have not passed through the hands of many different people over the course of unknown time. You can easily grow; you are mushrooms organically as well, which will save you from being exposed to any pesticides and fertilizers used by big companies. They taste much better than store-bought mushrooms because you freshly harvest them.

It's Cheaper to Grow Them

As we will discuss later, we will learn about the number of materials used to grow mushrooms and how they are extremely minimal, and the only major cost is buying the actual spawn used to grow the mushrooms. Growing mushrooms is also not a huge time consumer, so this is a wonderful hobby to partake in. You will quickly make your money back from your investment in materials to make mushrooms. Try out Shiitake mushrooms, which yield mushrooms for five years every five weeks after ONE sowing. That is a marvelous return on investment.

Growing Mushrooms is a Wonderful Activity

Growing mushrooms is a very interesting thing to start doing because not too many people are familiar with this idea of growing your own mushrooms. This does not mean, however, that there is not a large community of people that do partake in this activity. Growing your own mushrooms is an opportunity for education an opportunity to meet new people, and a wonderful way to take up a new hobby while helping the environment at the same time.

Another wonderful activity for the mushroom lover is to forage for mushrooms. We will talk later about the importance of good identification, and if you are able to do this, you will be able to enjoy this fantastic sport. Before cultivation happened, humans had to learn how to forage their own food. Since Jean-Jacques Paulet wrote the first book on edible mushrooms and how to identify them, identification books have advanced greatly, so you will be able to partake in this activity. Children used to actually get out of school early to help their parents in the field to survive the winter. Until recent globalization, mushroom foraging was a national pastime. Later on, we will talk about the cultivation of mushrooms, which was first written about by the botanist Pier Antonio Micheli in 1729.

Opportunity for Education

When it comes to growing your own food, it's impossible not to learn something about the process by which the thing is grown. You will learn about the life cycle of a mushroom, the role it has in the environment, and the overall importance of the mushroom in the ecosphere. You will also learn about the different types of mushrooms as well, and this will make for a grade school project for your kids or for the science fair coming up soon.

Meet New People

You will also learn a good deal of new people as you start to ask questions go to Growing workshops and pass on knowledge to younger Minds that are interested in getting into the process of growing your own food/mushrooms. Most people who are interested in this hobby are very friendly and willing to answer tough questions about what to do when first starting out like a mushroom grower.

Fun Hobby

Overall, growing mushrooms is an enjoyable hobby that most people do not partake in. You will learn many new things about mushrooms and their role in the environment, oh, and it will be an amazing pastime that doesn't take up too much of your time. You will get out as much as you put in when it comes to mushroom farming.

Growing Mushrooms will Improve You as a Person

Out of all of these points, mushrooms are just a wonderful thing to get into more, because they taste great, they help with you getting enough of your nutrients, and growing them is honestly just plain fun. As we mentioned earlier, you will get to know other great people that do the same thing as you, and you will learn much about nature itself through growing your own mushrooms, and that alone is going to change you for the better.

They Taste Great

From Puffballs to Portobello, from Shiitake to Oyster, there are plenty of different mushrooms to choose from. We all have our tastes, and by reading this book, it shows that you are interested in mushrooms, and that leads to the fact that you probably have a taste for mushrooms as well. Be sure to try out a few dozen different species before you knock them completely because many different types have different tastes and textures. You never know what a Button mushroom would taste like in comparison to a Jew's Ear mushroom (actual name), from a more solid fungus to a jelly mushroom. This will be your chance to learn about literally hundreds of different fungi over the course of your adventure.

It's Fun

Speaking from my own experience, growing your own anything is a wonderful experience, and the people I was able to interview for this book had nothing but good things to say about growing mushrooms. There is just something so magical about seeing mushrooms pop up from their substrate after a couple of weeks of growing. You see, after you see the primordial mushrooms sprout after a few weeks, you will have fully grown mushrooms. It just goes to show why people used to think that mushrooms were the result of lightning striking the earth in a specific place.

Missing Nutrients

Mushrooms are a wonderful source for fiber, protein, manganese, magnesium, iron, potassium, and many other important nutrients and elements that are wonderful to have in your stomach. They are a great addition to anyone's meal plan, especially when you are not eating meat. Mushrooms can replicate meats so well that vegetarians have been using them for years, and for thousands of years, monks that would fast from meat for a set amount of time would turn to mushrooms for a meat replacement.

Health Benefits of Mushrooms

While the exact health benefits are usually a bit divided between potential health benefits and empirically proven health benefits, most of the potential health benefits come from historically and anecdotal evidence from the East, such as China and Japan. We will focus on both of these types of health benefits. Both are well supported by data and opinions of people that have used mushrooms for their own benefit. They are used by vegans and meat-eaters alike. Overall, mushrooms are widely consumed as low cholesterol and low-calorie health-promoting food that is helpful in many different ways for all sorts of different people. According to a study (see references) on the recent developments in mushrooms as anti-cancer therapeutics, "The chief medicinal uses of mushrooms discovered so far are as antioxidant, anti-diabetic, hypocholesterolemic, anti-tumor, anti-cancer, immunomodulatory, anti-allergic, nephroprotective, and antimicrobial agents." Those are some big words, but we will get into the brass tacks of the situation and see what that all means for you.

In the scope of this section, we will talk about how mushrooms can help against diabetes (type 2 specifically), Alzheimer's, and cancer. There are plenty of reasons to start eating and using mushrooms for medicinal reasons, but these are perhaps the most important reasons. We will then go through the list of different vitamins and compounds in mushrooms that are helpful in each and every person's life, regardless of sex, age, or lifestyle. There is a massive number of different vitamins and antioxidants that will benefit you in many different ways.

Advocate for Heart Health, Protection against Diabetes

Mushrooms have been shown to have certain phytonutrients that can help prevent cells from sticking to vessel walls helping to lower cholesterol. This has been particularly helpful for overweight adults with type 2 diabetes. Mushrooms are a good source of vitamin C, potassium, fiber, and all of these elements have been known to contribute to good cardiovascular health. Current guidelines call for people to consume around 4,700 mg of potassium each day, while only one cup of mushrooms is known to have about 305 milligrams of potassium. This is why mushrooms should be part of your daily meal consumption, only adding to potential helpfulness.

According to study, the sort of fiber that is found in mushrooms may also help lower blood cholesterol. These sorts of fibers are called beta-glucans. Shiitake mushrooms are especially a good source of these nutrients, most notably in the stem of the mushroom. Mushrooms are also a great source of dietary fiber. A cup of raw mushrooms weigh approximately 78 G provides about 2 grams of fiber, and the American guidelines recommend that adults consume about 30 G of dietary fiber everyday fluctuating based on age and sex of the patient. This is helpful as a nutrient in many ways.

This dietary fiber is obviously helpful in managing type 2 diabetes, as well. For those who already have type 2, diabetes fiber has been known to reduce the level of glucose in the patient, a helpful element. Also, consuming a good amount of dietary fiber in your daily diet is known to reduce your risk of developing type 2 diabetes. So, whether you have it already or are worried about getting it, eating dietary fiber, of which mushrooms are a good source, is an overall helpful preventive measure. The International Journal of Medicinal Mushrooms found that a particular type of pink oyster mushrooms Health reduced total cholesterol and something called LDL "bad" cholesterol in certain types of rats. This goes to show that all mushrooms have low cholesterol inhibitors, but certain types of mushrooms are even more helpful in the fight against heart disease and type 2 diabetes.

Alzheimer's Disease and Dementia

Mushrooms are strangely effective at lowering seniors' risk of cognitive problems. A six-year study of over 600 adults over the age of 60 found that when these adults had two portions of mushrooms per day, there was a 50% decrease in the risk of mild cognitive impairment. A portion was about 150 grams of mushrooms or ¾ of a cup. In some cases, even one portion of cooked mushrooms would have a positive effect on the cognitive decline of elders. Mild cognitive impairment symptoms include not being able to do moderately easy tasks such as cooking a meal for brushing your teeth in the morning. Most doctors see this as the first signs of Alzheimer's, as half of these kinds of impairments lead to developing the disease later on in the patient's life. This study used a white button, shiitake, oyster, and golden mushrooms in their study. ET, or Ergothioneine, is the compound that is found naturally in mushrooms, but not naturally synthesized in humans, so obtaining this compound through their dietary sources is the most successful way to have this compound.

Protection Against Cancer

Multiple varieties of mushrooms have been shown to be able to protect against cancer by inhibiting tumor formation, the same way it prevents Alzheimer's in a more physical sense. This will help against DNA damage because of the actions against tumors early on in their development. According to the National Cancer Institute, the kinds of antioxidants found in mushrooms have been found to prevent breast, prostate, lung, and other types of cancer in recent studies. Vitamin D and Choline are both found abundantly in mushrooms of all kinds, and both have been found to prevent or treat most kinds of cancer, although the results may vary from person to person depending on the severity of the cancer of the patient.

According to a study published in the Journal of Experimental Biology and Medicine, after five different mushrooms were tested, of which were crimini, maitake, portabella, oyster, and white button, they found that the mushrooms suppressed breast cancer growth in certain patients in a very significant way. Shiitake mushrooms actually have something called lentinan, which has been known to extend the survival rate of patients when used with chemotherapy.

Lastly, Clinical trials done at the John Hopkins University School of Medicine used psilocybin, the naturally occurring psychedelic compounds found in hundreds of different types of mushrooms, on a number of different patients that were struggling with anxiety, depression, and fear as they were dying of cancer. 80% of patients had an increasing sense of optimism connection with other people and even spiritual experiences because of the drug. This suggests that psilocybin could be beneficial for people who are struggling with depression or PTSD.

Help with Pregnancy

During pregnancy, folic acid (folate) is used by women to promote fetal health, and mushrooms are actually full of this B-9 vitamin. One cup of raw mushrooms contains 16 MCG of folate, while the current guidelines have us consuming around 400 MCG each day.

Nutrient	Amount of nutrient in 1 cup of mushrooms	Recommended daily intake Trusted Source
Energy (calories)	21.1	1,600–3,200
Protein (g)	3.0	46–56
Carbohydrate (g)	3.1, including 1.9 g of sugar	130
Calcium (mg)	2.9	1,000–1,300
Iron (mg)	0.5	8–18

Magnesium (mg)	8.6	310–420
Phosphorus (mg)	82.6	700–1,250
Potassium (mg)	305	4,700
Sodium (mg)	4.8	2,300
Zinc (mg)	0.5	8–11
Copper (mcg)	305	890–900
Selenium (mcg)	8.9	55
Vitamin C (mg)	2.0	65–90
Vitamin D (mg)	0.2	15
Folate (mcg DFE)	16.3	400
Choline (mg)	16.6	400–550
Niacin (mg)	3.5	14–16

Chart from
https://www.medicalnewstoday.com/articles/278858.php#nutrition

CHAPTER 3

MUSHROOM BASICS

This section of the book should be very helpful for you in your exploration of mushrooms themselves. There are plenty of things to know about mushrooms, and hopefully, this short guide will give you the resources you need to become a more professional mushroom grower.

What is a Mushroom?

Most people will class a mushroom as a vegetable, but it isn't. Every fruit and every vegetable comes from an edible plant. And each of those plants shares one common characteristic – they all contain chlorophyll. This is used to convert the sunlight that falls on the plants into carbohydrates.

Mushrooms do not have any chlorophyll and cannot photosynthesize; instead, a mushroom will steal the carbohydrates it requires from other plants. Mushrooms are classed as fungi, one of many different species and, because there are so many species, they even have their own kingdom now, "the kingdom of fungi."

Mushroom Ecology

We can divide fungi into three separate categories, based on the relationship they have with other plants:

1. **Saprophytes** – these are found growing on plant roots, fallen leaves, dead wood, and other organic, dead matter. They take minerals and carbon dioxide from this organic matter, and the category includes medicinal and gourmet mushrooms, such as the cremini, white button, oyster, and shiitake.
2. **Parasites** – these are found growing on living plants and trees and extract nutrients from them. Because of this, they are known as "murderers"; when the living matter has died, the saprophytes move in to clean up.
3. **Mycorrhiza** – these form symbiotic relationships with living tree roots, extracting nutrients, and sugars. However, they also help to enlarge the tree root system by giving back essential elements and minerals. This is a problematic category of mushroom to cultivate and are usually only found in the wild. The class contains truffles, chanterelles, and porcini mushrooms.

Mushrooms begin life as white fluff beneath the ground. This is known as mycelium, fungal threads from which the mushrooms sprout. Mushrooms are fruits from bigger fungi that grow beneath the ground.

In nature, mycelium can remain beneath the ground for long periods, not emerging until the conditions are favorable. Those conditions include temperature, humidity, and food sources. When everything is in favor, small buds form, pushing up to find daylight, and a mushroom is born. The small ball is normally white and quickly grows to a proper form. The cap opens, and millions of spores are dropped, picked up by the wind and dropped elsewhere, where they begin the task of forming more mycelium.

Parts of a Mushroom

In preparation for growing your own mushrooms, it is very helpful to know all the parts of the mushroom to understand their anatomy and growth periods. This will make you a more effective and professional grower. You will also have the skills to identify mushrooms much easier if you understand all the parts to the mushroom. These parts include the spores, the stem, gills, mycelium, hyphae, volva, and the cap. Refer back to this section when you are ever confused about mushroom identification guides. Pros made these guides, so be sure to read them carefully; you are able to learn a lot from them.

Spores

The spores are the agents of reproduction for the mushroom. A single mushroom colony is able to produce millions of fungal spores into the biosphere in a single meter of air. They are extremely small compared to regular seeds produced by plants, spores typically being 1/100 of a millimeter long, and are designed specifically for wind transportation. There are many different types of spores, as they vary in size, shape, color, and other variations that aid them in their conquest of different territories around the world. One fungus, the *Coprophilous Fungi* (literally named the "dung-loving fungi), is a type of saprobic fungi that grows specifically on animal dung. *Huitlacoche* is a fungus that only grows on ears of corn(actually considered to be a delicacy among Native Americans and they even used it as a topping for their tortillas after scraping it off the ears of corn the fungi would grow on), and *Inonotus obliquus* is a type that grows on birch trees in colder climates. Each type of spore has a specific goal in its creation, so mycology seeks to understand these distinctions.

Mushrooms are known as an iteroparous organism, meaning that they produce offspring more than once in a lifetime. In fact, the mushrooms should be in their own category because they so blatantly destroy this definition by producing trillion of reproducing cells over their lifetime. Many spores are, in fact, sent out, but many do not survive. This is why you only see a handful of puffballs in a meadow instead of covering the entire field. The spores may be eaten by slugs, springtails, worms, or any other small predators as they attempt to mature into a mushroom that can complete the circle of life. The mushroom also needs to be wary of competition created by its own showering of spores when searching for food to survive on. The mushroom has prepared for this, of course. Most of the resources of the fungi are loaded into the reproduction element of its being to create as many spores as possible to get them to where they need to be.

Stem

This part of the mushroom is simply the part that supports the cap of the mushroom. In mycology, it is also commonly referred to as the stipe. This part of the mushroom is important in three respects, and I will list them now.

First, it is important as an axis to hold up the cap of the mushroom itself, so that the mushroom is able to work as it is supposed to. Without this part of the mushroom, the cap would be resting on the meadow or forest floor so that it would be exposed to more of the elements. Secondly, the stem is considered to be the mediating factor in spore dispersal. The angle at which the cap is pointed will either make it harder or easier to release spores into the wind currents. However, it is important to note that not all mushrooms even have this feature, such as the puffball, smuts, and jelly fungi. Lastly, the stipe is considered to be very important in making a correct identification of a mushroom, counting such characteristics as: the texture of the stipe, the general size and shape, the color of the stipe, whether it has something called a or a universal veil (volva), and whether the stipe extends underground such as with a rhizome.

Gill

Most of the mushrooms you are most likely familiar with are gilled mushrooms. These gills are papery structures that extend off of the cap of the mushroom that has the sole purpose of producing spores. You could say that this is the most important job in the mushroom because, without these spores, there are no mushroom colonies. Attributes such as how the gill is attached to the stem, the color of the gills and the bruising color that is made when they are disturbed, gill spacing (this one is a bit more subjective but still helpful in overall observations), and length can call lead an avid mushroomer to identify what kind of mushroom they are looking at.

Mycelium

This is the vegetative part of a mushroom colony, the mass of branching hyphae, which is discussed after this section. This mechanism of the mushroom helps absorb nutrients from the ground in order for the mushroom colony to create fruiting bodies or the shapes that we are familiar with when it comes to mushrooms. The Mycelium is what is so beneficial when it comes to the health of the forest and aquatic ecosystems for the role they play in the decomposition of plant and animal material. They contribute to the carbon cycle by releasing carbon dioxide back into the atmosphere as they break down materials into usable soil.

This part of the mushroom is also extremely important to consider when growing your own mushrooms because of the grower needing to be aware of the types of nutrients that are needed to grow certain mushrooms you are targeting, as well as assessing the overall health of the mushroom. Mycelium will either look like an aboveground rooting system or a collection of white mass spreading out from the center of the spore bed it has created.

Hypha

Hyphae are the long, branching agents that collectively make up the mycelium. Think of a tree as mycelium and the individual branches as hyphae. These branches are the main proponent for vegetative growth for mushroom or overall fungi. They spread over pockets of nutrients, and then continue to spread to find more pockets, never being satisfied with their lot.

Volva

This is the remnant of an egg-like, cup-shape part of the peridium of a mushroom that enclosed the immature fruiting body of many fungi. Its most important feature is it's helpful in the identification of poisonous and non-poisonous mushrooms, given that many poisonous mushrooms are contained within a family that has this feature. The Volva is usually completely or partially buried underground, so be warned all potential foragers. Identification guides will take special notice of this part of the mushroom.

Cap

This is the most important in identifying what kind of mushroom you are dealing with. Its main goal is in the protection of the gills and spores just below it, acting as a wall between the outside world and the spores before the stem twists in such a way as to allow the millions of spores to travel to where they need to go.

MUSHROOMS

Species	Fresh weight (x 1,000 t)				Increase %
	1986		1997		
Agaricus bisporus	1,227	(56.2%)	1,956	(31.8%)	59.4
Lentinula edodes	314	(14.4%)	1,564	(25.4%)	398.1
Pleurotus spp.	169	(7.7%)	876	(14.2%)	418.3
Auricularia spp.	119	(5.5%)	485	(7.9%)	307.6
Volvariella volvacea	178	(8.2%)	181	(3.0%)	1.7
Flammulina velutipes	100	(4.6%)	285	(4.6%)	130.0
Tremella fuciformis	40	(1.8%)	130	(2.1%)	225.0
Hypsizygus marmoreus	-	-	74	(1.2%)	-
Pholiota nameko	25	(1.1%)	56	(0.9%)	124.0
Grifola frondosa	-	-	33	(0.5%)	-
Others	10	(0.5%)	518	(8.4%)	5,080.0
Total	2,182	(100.0%)	6,158	(100.0%)	182.2

Adapted from Penn State.

Life Cycle of Mushrooms

The life cycle of the mushrooms remains mostly invisible for most of us, but not with cultivators. If you are getting into growing mushrooms, then you will be shocked at how much you are going to learn when it comes to the overall life of a mushroom. By knowing all the parts to the mushroom life cycle, you will be able to figure out what is wrong with your mushrooms if they are failing to produce, and you will be able to fix the problem because of your extensive knowledge on the subject. It also forces you to learn the terminology that you would most likely ignore, and knowing these terms will help you become a better hunter and ID'er.

1. Inoculation

When spores are released from the mushroom, they fall upon the right substrate or growing medium, and if the conditions are extremely favorable, the spores will germinate and start to grow. There are many circumstances in which mushrooms will not form properly, and this is why there are millions of spores that are released from the mushroom to find a suitable location to host.

2. Spore Germination

Hyphae, as we discussed earlier, will start to grow from the spores. These hyphae start to work together to create mycelium. Nutrients will start to be absorbed and collect into the center of the mushrooms colony to start creating more hyphae and eventually make a fruiting body, which we usually call a mushroom.

3. Mycelial Expansion

Mycelium is a large network of cells that works to provide nutrients for the whole mushroom. The mushroom we normally think of, a cap and stem, is actually the fruit of the organism, while the mycelium is the plant that works to supply the fruit body with nutrients. As the mycelium develops, it breaks down nearby organic matter and absorbs nutrients from its surroundings. The mycelium will then start to grow at an exponential rate as it goes up against a large number of predators nearby. It will then use many different enzymes and compounds in which to repel these predators and competitors, such as the immune system does for humans and other organisms.

4. Primordia

Mycelium then forms into hyphal knots in crowded areas in the mycelium expansion, also called primordia. This is always a welcome sign to any mushroom cultivator or grower because it means that mushrooms will soon be appearing in the near future. Primordia are also known as baby mushrooms.

5. Primordia Formation

The mushroom organism then produces more enzymes and optimizes both the mycelium and fruit body. This is the stage where much of the nutrients, antioxidants, and other good health benefits are formed, so this is a very important part of the overall process of growing mushrooms. If something were to happen to the mushroom at this stage, it would lose out on many different health benefits, so be careful at this stage in mushroom development when you are growing them.

6. Fruitbody Selection

From the millions of different primordia, the growing organism has to select the most promising primordia to allow them to grow to maturity and thus bring about the rest of the DNA to new organisms.

7. Mature Fruit Body

The new organism channels all of its energy to develop the mature fruit body. This will finally be able to produce spores that are needed to reproduce more mushrooms in the future sexually. This is the chief end of the mushroom life cycle, as in the next phase, the spores will be released.

8. Spore Release

The spores are then released into the environment, looking for a suitable substrate on which to grow and start the cycle all over again.

CHAPTER 4
GROWING MUSHROOMS

This is the amazing next step for anyone that is interested in mushrooms! I hope that my readers can get to this step and start the process of growing their own mushrooms. Here I will lay out several different mushrooms that you can grow on your own as well as the most popular ways to grow your mushrooms yourselves.

Common Mushrooms to Grow

Here I have provided a list of mushrooms that are common to grow and within reason to be easy ones to grow as well.

Maitake

What It Is

Its Latin name is *Grifola Frondosa; this* mushroom grows at the base of trees, those trees mostly being oaks in early autumn. This is what is known as a cluster mushroom, given how it grows in such a way. It is also a very large mushroom in comparison to others on this list. Maitake means Dancing Mushroom in its native origin of Japan, which is said to have been named after it was discovered in the woods and the people who discovered it dance with happiness because of its healing properties. It is also called the Hen of the Woods because of what it looks like.

Where it is grown/Seasons

This mushroom grows wildly in most of China and Japan, and in parts of the North American continent. It can be found in the wild around Oak and Maple trees and sometimes Elm trees in the autumn months. It grows best in the wild but can also be used at home. At home, it grows best in grow bags with the correct substrate (straw is best for this and most other mushrooms).

What it is used for

These mushrooms have equal use as a medicine and supplement as they do a portion of food for famous restaurants and tasty dishes. It has shown to lower cholesterol and be effective in fighting against cancer. So, it is effective at helping against type 2 diabetes as well as destroying cancer cells.

Taste

It goes well in soups because of its powerful umami flavor. These are some of the most sought after mushrooms for their taste and many health benefits. It also goes well as a soup stock from personal experience. Being cooked in foil with butter is also a great way to eat them. There are plenty of different ways to cook this mushroom, but this is one of the best and easiest ways to do so.

Health Benefits

Many more studies are needed to understand its effects on humans, but research is very promising with maitake mushroom. It has shown the ability to fight cancer and destroy cancer cells, lower cholesterol, and having a positive effect on type 2 diabetes as well. Also, they are overall very effective in improving the function of the immune system and regulating blood pressure.

How to Grow + Ease of Growth

These are a bit difficult to grow, but substrate in a grow bag is the most effective way to grow this mushroom. The fruit in later summer through the fall, so room temperature inside seems to be the most effective way to grow them. They are relatively difficult to grow but well worth the hassle.

Unique Facts of Each

They can get to up to 25 pounds or so on average, being a very large fungus. They have also been known to get up to 100 lbs in Japan, becoming known as the "King of Mushrooms."

They are one of the most sought after culinary-type mushrooms in the world.

MUSHROOMS

These are most famously known for their cancer-fighting ability.

Maitake Mushrooms (see above)

Enoki

<u>What It Is</u>

Flammulina velutipes is a well-known part of Japanese cooking, commercially farmed as long, white mushrooms that have a distinctive crunch to them. They are also known as Golden Needle mushrooms or Futu Mushrooms. They range from being red to white, depending on the level of cultivation that has occurred.

Where it is grown/ Seasons

It is native to Japan but can easily be grown indoors in any season. It does best in the fall and can be found around the North American continent now because of European traders and travelers bringing them over with them as they migrated to the Americas.

What it is used for

It is mostly used as a culinary mushroom, being used in soups, salads, and other dishes. They, like most other mushrooms, are a wonderful source of antioxidants.

Taste

They have a delicate, crunchy taste that is very distinctive. This mushroom is a wonderful addition to any stir fry or soup. They go great with garlic and scallion sauce, as well as with shrimp. A few of the recipes listed below use this mushroom.

Health Benefits

This mushroom, like most, is full of antioxidants and has been used on animals to inhibit cancer growth and in the development of certain vaccines. This antioxidant called ergothioneine can be taken orally for extra health benefits and concentration of the antioxidant.

MUSHROOMS

How to Grow + Ease of Growth

Many starter kits help you grow these small mushrooms, so try one of them out and keep them in the dark and dank area where they can flourish. Many growers use water bottles and are grown in a sawdust substrate. Follow the steps provided in a later chapter. Just be sure to keep the humidity very high for the early stages.

Unique Facts of Each

They look completely different in the wild from the cultivated adaptations of themselves. Humans have completely changed them for their own purposes.

These mushrooms tend to take longer to mature, about 90 days after you begin growing them.

MUSHROOMS

Enoki (see above)

Oyster

<u>What It Is</u>

Also known as *Pleurotus ostreatus*, these are some of the most common mushrooms to be cultivated in the world. They can also be called pearl oyster mushrooms or tree oyster mushrooms.

<u>History of Mushroom</u>

MUSHROOMS

First cultivated by German soldiers during WW2, there has been an outstanding increase in the number of mushrooms sold around the world. This is because they are very easy to cultivate yield a massive number of mushrooms with a small amount of work added to them. We will go through the specifics later in this book.

Where it is grown/ Seasons

These are able to be grown every season in different parts of the world, and they are known to be a very good indoor crop to grow for novice mushroom growers. They are now found naturally in the Americas for their hardiness and ability to withstand cold weather.

What it is used for

The most popular use for mushrooms is to sauté or stir-fry them, especially with butter and oil under very high heat. They are wonderful as a topping for toast, in pasta, sauces, and risotto. There are also a rising number of health benefits for oyster mushrooms in the western world of science, many of which focus on cancer and virus research.

Taste

They are a beloved favorite for their mild and savory flavor that goes with basically any dish. They go wonderfully in a sauté with garlic and green onions with a bit of oil. Once they turn golden brown, they are ready to go. There is also a very strong earthy taste to them because of their mild flavor. Frying, roasting, and grilling are all great choices with this mushroom because they tend to hold up their texture under extreme heat. Keep in mind that they are about 80% water and will shrink when they are cooked, so don't be surprised when they change shape dramatically. A few of the recipes listed below use this mushroom.

Health Benefits

One cup of raw oyster mushrooms has about 30 calories and 4 grams of protein, a stable in a vegan and vegetarian lifestyle. They have many vitamins, including phosphorus, copper, and potassium. There is a small bit of research that claims that they inhibit the growth of cancer cells, much like other mushrooms. They also help to boost the immune system and provide ample strength against viruses. For being one of the more common mushrooms, they are also dramatically one of the best mushrooms for your immune system.

How to Grow + Ease of Growth

The process by which people grow oyster mushrooms is outlined in a later chapter, and the reason this is the most common cultivated mushroom is because of the fast production methods and benefits associated with growing these mushrooms. They grow extremely fast and have a huge yield at the end of their growing period. This mushroom is good for beginners and veterans.

Unique Facts of Each

MUSHROOMS

There are many oyster mushrooms in the wild, but they were first cultivated by the Germans during WW2 to be used as extra rations during the failing war effort.

There has been an increase of about 18-fold between the years 1965 and 1997 for the production of oyster mushrooms because of faster production methods and the interest in health benefits associated with these mushrooms.

Oyster Mushroom (see above)

Shiitake

<u>What It Is</u>

The Latin name being *Lentunula Edodes*, these are one of the most famous mushrooms in the world, and for a good reason.

History of Mushroom

Shiitake has historically been used as a mouth rinse for dental plaque, as welled to treat HIV/AIDS and eczema. Also known as the Forest mushroom or the Champignon Noir. This mushroom was used by monks as a meat substitute when they fasted from meat for religious reasons.

Where it is grown/ Seasons

They are native to Asia, with different species grow at different times of the year, some in the cold and some in the warm.

What it is used for

They are used in many fancy dishes in Japan as well as common dishes such as salads and soups, and they are used as a supplement for cancer patients in China. They are a huge source of vitamin D if harvested correctly, as well.

Taste

They are extremely meaty, with a mild flavor that is close to Umami. This is a truly delicious mushroom. This is a wonderful mushroom to have when you are fasting from meat or going vegan. A few of the recipes listed below use this mushroom.

Health Benefits

These mushrooms have been shown to lower cholesterol, help with weight loss, and boost the immune system. One of the most helpful and delicious mushrooms out there. They are also low in calories and sodium, having plenty of B vitamins as well.

How to Grow + Ease of Growth

These mushrooms are a bit more challenging to grow because their mycelium is not as easy to grow as varieties such as oyster mushrooms, but the result is well worth it if you put the time in to see them through. They grow in flushes, meaning they continue to produce after you first plant them, sometimes for years and years under the right conditions. The most important thing to remember when growing these mushrooms is that they a wood-based substrate to grow properly.

Unique Facts of Each

Shiitake mushrooms can produce every five weeks for five years if done right.

Shiitake mushrooms grow best on fresh logs.

Submerge the logs you plan on planting in cold water for a full day.

MUSHROOMS

You can drastically boost the vitamin D content in your shiitake mushrooms by putting them gill side up in a sunny location for 24 to 48 hours after you harvest them.

Shiitake Mushrooms (see above)

Lion's Mane

<u>What It Is</u>

Under the name, *Hericium Erinaceus*, this mushroom is also known as satyr's beard, bearded hedgehog, pom-pom mushroom, monkey's head mushroom, and many other names. It is edible as well as medicinal.

<u>History of Mushroom</u>

Native Americans were first known to use this mushroom for medical purposes.

Where it is grown/ Seasons

It is native to North America as well as Europe and Asia, and it grows during late summer on mainly American Beech trees. It comes with no distinct cap, lacks a stipe, and is parasitic.

What it is used for

Mostly used for medical purposes, it also has been used as a substitute for seafood.

Taste

Many people call the flavor a bit like seafood, such as a lobster taste. Lions Mane is a good meat substitute.

Health Benefits

One of the most well-known health benefits to these fungi is their ability to fight against dementia and overall fight for cognitive health. Two special compounds, hericenones and erinacines, are known to stimulate the growth of brain cells. This mushroom has also been wonderful in its effectiveness against depression and anxiety in patients with chronic inflammation. Other health benefits include protection against ulcers, reduction of heart disease risks, management of diabetic symptoms, and boosting the immune system.

How to Grow + Ease of Growth

The best way to grow one of these mushrooms is to buy a kit and start that way. They are actually very easy to grow and tend to produce a few rounds of mushrooms, just make sure that you are watching their humidity.

Unique Facts of Each

This mushroom looks just like a lion's mane.

Native Americans used this as a substitute for seafood in more North-Eastern tribes.

MUSHROOMS

Lion's Mane (see above)

Wine Cap

<u>What It Is</u>

Also known as *Stropharia rugoso-annulata*, these mushrooms are mostly eaten when they are very young. According to leading mycologists, the white cap mushroom has no poisonous look-alikes, so this mushroom is relatively easy to forge, but always use proper precautions. They also have the name "Godzilla Mushroom."

MUSHROOMS

History of Mushroom

They are historically known to be used to enrich Gardens by providing protein through their mycelium. These mushrooms are first cultivated in the late 1960s in Germany and can be found in Farmers markers in all parts of the United States as well as Europe Asia and even New Zealand.

Where it is grown/ Seasons

These mushrooms flourish around late spring and early fall but can be grown indoors all year round.

What it is used for

There are many uses for wine cap mushrooms. They are most commonly used in grilling and sautéing, and when they are young, they can be used because of their texture in stir-fries. They pair exceptionally well with nutmeg, quinoa, pasta, lemon, and wine. They can be served with meat (especially fish) and added to soups and salads.

Taste

The stems can be cooked to a crispy flavor, and have a mild and earthy, nutty flavor that tastes somewhat of red wine, giving it its name. Some people even say that it tastes somewhat like potatoes, but I digress.

Health Benefits

Wine cap mushrooms are a great provider of fiber and vitamin D, in addition to as protein copper and some calcium as well.

How to Grow + Ease of Growth

These mushrooms are most commonly grown in home gardens, oh, and they are very easy to grow if you have the right substrate. They grow best with straw and sawdust and can be used to benefit other vegetables in your gardens, such as corn or wheat.

Unique Facts of Each

They will keep for up to a week if stored in a refrigerator after harvest.

They have a very unusual flavor, and that is why it is so popular for chefs to use in their dishes.

When it is young, the cap will be a bit purple but will become brownish overtime. You should also get a purple spore print if you choose to do one of those.

MUSHROOMS

Growing a Mushroom

This activity is a deeply satisfying one, and I am excited for you to start trying out the art of growing your own food or medicine. It is truly a fulfilling thing to provide for oneself, so read the next section carefully so that you can do the right things to provide the most mushrooms possible for your ability. We start by laying down a substrate, pasteurization of the soil, incubation, and then finally harvesting. This whole process should take around a few weeks.

For this example, we will discuss how to grow specifically an oyster mushroom, one of the easiest mushrooms to grow. Many of these tips apply to all mushrooms for cultivation, so feel free to use this guide for other types of mushrooms as well.

Sow: Substrate and Container

It should be obvious to you now that mushrooms feed on organic matter. They do not need the sun, such as plants, because they do not have the right cells for photosynthesis to occur. Plants have chloroplasts and can make their own food while mushrooms are heterotrophic, meaning they are not able to make their own food, but instead need their food from existing sources of plant and animal matter.

This is where the substrate comes in. The word substrate is extremely broad, but in this example, it relates to the organic material used to grow mushrooms on. Most substrates are full of nitrogen and excellent for overall plant growth. These are known as "Greens" when it comes to composting, such as peat moss, manure, hay, cocoa seeds, coffee grounds, grass clippings, etc. The best option for a beginner is anything inexpensive and local, so you can cut down on any invaders. **Straw is probably the best pick for any level.**

As for the container that you use, there are hundreds of different choices, such as a laundry basket, a potato sack, a box, a pair of shoes, a bucket, etc. Just make sure that the container has holes that allow for drainage of water as well as aeration for oxygen flow.

This is why mushrooms are so extremely sustainable; they can literally be grown in dung. Growers just need to make sure that the substrate they are using is full of nitrogen, at a good and neutral pH level, and properly fermented at a temperature of around 170 F. At this point, the compost substrate should look very brown and smell like ammonia. This leads us to pasteurization.

Steam Pasteurization

To alleviate the troubles of pests and unwanted fungi invaders, the best thing to do is to treat the substrate by exposing it to hot water or steam to pasteurize it. Without doing this, your harvests will be sporadic and inconsistent. The ammonia that was created in phase one should be used by good microbes to make a protein that is helpful for mushrooms to be food for the mushrooms. You can place your substrate in a pillowcase and allow boiling water to kill the rest of the microbes inside the substrate. The substrate can then be allowed to dry off. Eliminate as much water as possible, because leaving any extra water in the substrate will not be helpful to the growth of mushrooms.

Next, you need to make sure your substrate is safe by decontaminating all surfaces you have touched and then lay the substrate on the table you are using to bring it all down to room temperature.

Spawn and its Issues

Mycelium will be produced from the billions of spores that are released by the mushrooms inside your substrate to create spawn. You will inoculate your substrate by adding the spawn to the substrate. Put the spawn in a clean bucket as you wait for the substrate to cool. Immediately afterward, alternate 1 to 2 inches of the substrate with .5

inches of spawn. Mix and repeat. The spawn should be on top. You can also mix the substrate and spawn so that the spawn is on top and then spread the mixture around and put it in the container you have chosen You then need to make sure that you are maintaining moisture inside of the mixture, as mycelium spreads and grows over the substrate (this is also called colonization).

Incubation

You can do this by putting your container in a trash bag, keeping the top open so that air can move around inside of the container, and then put the bag in a dark area that stays at a consistent 60-85 degrees F. After two weeks you should start to see small mushrooms called primordia forming, and then you should move your mushrooms to a new suitable location.

Conditions for a New Location

Here is a shortlist of conditions that are important in the creation of mushrooms at this stage, and if any of these conditions are not met, then you will have less than perfect mushrooms.

- Light: You need enough light so that you can read in it but not in direct sunlight

- Temperature: 60-80 degrees

- Humility: High. This will result in much bigger mushrooms, so be sure to cover your container with a clear trash bag to still allow for aeration but keep the heat and water moisture inside. Mist water 1-2 times a day inside the bag.

- Airflow: Cut about a dozen half-inch holes in the bag to create a good airflow for the mushrooms

Harvest

About 3-5 days after your primordia sprout, you should be ready to harvest. Mushrooms tend to grow exponentially, meaning that once they hit a certain growth, they expand out wildly. Oyster mushrooms grow in clusters, and once the largest mushroom has an upward curve to it, that is an indication that the mushroom is ready to be harvested. This is because the mushroom is getting ready to release its spores.

Different Ways to Grow Mushrooms

You can grow your own mushrooms from scratch!

Buy some white button or oyster mushrooms from the store. Then you need to get your hands on some coffee grounds and then boil the grounds for about 20 minutes to make sure they are sterilized. Make sure that your hands are clean as well to guard against cross-containments.

Pour a good amount of coffee grounds into the jar that you have prepared. You can put the coffee ground as well as the filter right into the mixture; the mycelium will go right through the paper. Make sure that you are applying rubbing alcohol to EVERYTHING; on your hands, the jars, the coffee filters, your hands again. EVERYTHING

EVERY TIME. **You want as much sterility as possible for the mushrooms to grow effectively. This is the most important part of growing your own mushrooms.** You will put the mushrooms into the jars with coffee grounds covered by a coffee filter and a cap. Before this, however, you need to cut off the stem butt, or the bottom of the stem and then plant them into the coffee mixture. Make sure that the mycelium part is facing downwards towards the coffee grounds. The lid with the coffee filter will allow for proper airflow. After about eight days, you can then cover the mycelium with another layer of coffee grounds. Try to smother the mycelium, but allow it to be covered so that the mycelium can spread. Repeat this process until the jar is completely filled.

To clearly identify contamination, which is known as green mold, it will start off really small and then will spread out throughout the whole container if the green mold is not removed in time. This mold will attack the mycelium and destroy the colony. A good way to mitigate this damage to have about a dozen colonies of mycelium in a dozen different jars at a time to be most effective. It might be helpful to put some straw in your mixture of coffee grounds to make the situation go a bit faster.

Now, you will be able to separate the mycelium from the jar and transfer it to the straw. First, you need to cut your straw into quarter-inch lines and pour the straw into a bucket to sterilize it with hot water. You should make sure to submerge the straw completely, and then push the substrate down for a while, making sure the temperature is around 160. Always feel able to add more hot water to the substrate to keep the temperature where it needs to be. You will then remove the substrate from the water and make sure the substrate straw is nice and dry. You can use a variety of products to do this. You will then wipe down a plastic bag and fill it with the straw and then the mycelium that you have been growing. Open up the jar and pour the contents onto a plate to get the whole mycelium and coffee ground mixture out. You can tell it is ready on the coffee grounds now smell like mushrooms.

Place layer by layer of mycelium and straw at a time to make sure that the mushroom has a consistent place to go in. Poke holes in the bag to allow for aeration to occur and where the mushrooms will come out. Mist the bag every day once or twice to give it the best chance to grow.

CHAPTER 5
WAYS TO USE MUSHROOMS

This chapter by no means holds an exhaustive list of all the benefits of using mushrooms in your daily life, but it is truly a wonderful start. This information has been sourced out to many different scientific studies and professional surveys, so you can know you are getting the best information research has to offer. We will first go through a list of more than 40 ways to use and benefit from mushrooms, and then we will talk about a good number of recipes that mushrooms can be used for. Listing the benefits of mushrooms, in general, is a bit like listing the benefits of eating animals or vegetables. Because the subject matter is so broad, and there are over 200 edible species of mushrooms in the world, of course, there are so many benefits to mushrooms and using them in your personal life. This, of course, does not take away from the fact that mushrooms are extremely healthy for you as plants and animals are for you, and as processed foods are not overall good for you.

A List of Benefits

There are plenty of different ways to use mushrooms, whether it be for healing, eating, cooking for others, or disease prevention. It's no wonder why so many Eastern cultures have glorified mushrooms to such a degree. They are used in every culture from Native American to Japanese culture, from Norwegian to Icelandic cultures. This chapter will consist of a list of 42 uses for mushrooms, with information gathered from many different scholars, articles, research projects, and scientific studies. This list will be all you ever need when it comes to what you can use mushrooms for.

There is no particular order to this list, but all of these objects have been researched well and found to be true through anecdotal evidence as well. It is safe to say that all of these have been tested by multiple people, myself included, and that has allowed them to be on this list of about 43 uses and benefits for mushrooms. There are plenty more uses and reasons to grow mushrooms, but I hope that these will help you to see the reason why you should grow them in the first place. Even one of these reasons, taken in isolation, is a good enough reason for you to put these mushrooms on your shelf and get ready to use them and grow them. If you have any further questions, there should be a good amount of research done on the subject online if you are interested.

Here is a shortened list of the benefits thus listed below for your previewing. Hopefully, this will help you in finding what you are looking for quicker.

MUSHROOMS

1. Fights Against Hair Loss
2. Restores the Color of Your Hair
3. Get Rid of Dandruff
4. Lowering Cholesterol
5. Fighting Breast Cancer
6. Diabetic Diets
7. Building the Immune System
8. Helping with Weight Loss
9. Source of Vitamin B1
10. Source of Vitamin B2
11. Source of Vitamin D
12. Source of Vitamin B3
13. Source of Vitamin B5
14. Source of Vitamin B6
15. Source of Vitamin B9
16. Source of Vitamin H
17. Treatment of Skin Conditions
18. Fighting Against Aging
19. Helps Treat Acne
20. Helps Lighten Hair
21. Hydration of Skin
22. Destruction of Cancer Cells
23. Destruction of Viruses and Bacteria
24. Cleaning Polluted Soil
25. Restoration of Habitats by Polluting Factories
26. Potential Source of Fuel?
27. Used Instead of Styrofoam
28. Killing Kings
29. Promotion of Heart Health
30. Boiling
31. Frying

32. Stir Fry
33. Raw
34. Grilling
35. Sautéing
36. Help Support Liver and Kidney Function in Your Pets
37. Prevent Viral Infections in Your Pets
38. Contains Many Antioxidants
39. Garnish
40. Can produce Chitin
41. Turn Waste into Food
42. Teeth Health
43. Making Beer, Wine, and Bread

1. Fights against Hair Loss:

Mushrooms are a great source of iron, the main combatant against hair loss. This is an important mineral in the formation of red blood cells, which will, in turn, strengthen your hair cells. This fights against something called Anemia, which is the leading reason people lose their hair over time, because of a deficiency of iron in your blood. Mushrooms are great for a lot of reasons, and I bet you didn't know about this one!

2. Restores the Color of Your Hair

Because of the wonderful supply of copper in your mushrooms, this will help with the production of a pigment called melanin, which is the pigment that colors your hair. This, paired with the iron that we discussed earlier, promote strong and lively hair. Another benefit of why mushrooms are great for your hair, but that's not all.

3. Get Rid of Dandruff

Selenium is a huge part of mushrooms, and it is wonderfully effective against dandruff. This nutrient is mostly found in animals and is a very good alternative for all vegetarians to get this nutrient for their own benefit and healthy hair. As someone with a good amount of dandruff, I have found this one very helpful for dry and itchy hair.

4. Lowering Cholesterol

Many of the mushrooms that I have listed are extremely effective in lowering cholesterol in both lab tests as well as real applications on humans, so give mushrooms a try if you are struggling with your weight or heart disease.

5. Fights against Breast Cancer

Button mushrooms are extremely helpful in lowering the level of estrogen in your body so that you will be safer from breast cancer. They also suppress the level of activity of testosterone. In point 22, we will see how mushrooms help destroy cancer cells in general.

6. Diabetic Diets

Mushrooms are a wonderful source of dietary fiber, which has been known to help mitigate a number of health conditions, one of them being type 2 diabetes, given that they help lower blood glucose levels. In one cup of sliced mushrooms, there is around 1 gram of dietary fiber. 22 grams a day is recommended for adults to consume each day, so a few cups of mushrooms will give you a good boost to start your day off well.

7. Building the Immune System

Mushrooms are a wonderful choice for anyone looking to strengthen their immune system. A prime candidate for this would be the oyster mushroom, which helps drastically for this purpose. This is **probably the most useful part of mushrooms overall.** They are so packed full of nutrients that it is almost impossible to quantify how useful they are.

8. Helping with Weight Loss

Although there are few points of research to support this claim, it follows that while mushrooms are able to help regulate blood sugar and lower cholesterol levels, they should be able to contribute to weight loss in a wonderful way. Refer to points 4 and 6 on how mushrooms tend to be good for lowering cholesterol and for diabetic diets as well.

9. Source of Vitamin B1

Thiamine, also known as vitamin B1, is a wonderful additive to any diet. The shortage of Thiamine tends to create a loss of appetite, fatigue, blurry vision, vomiting, and even muscle weakness. It has been used to treat Alzheimer's disease, cataracts, and kidney disease.

Thiamine can also be found in pork, poultry, bread, rice, and yeast.

10. Source of Vitamin B2

Riboflavin, also known as vitamin B2, is a vitamin found naturally in food such as eggs, green vegetables, and milk. Riboflavin is commonly taken to help prevent cancer, headaches, muscle cramps, multiple sclerosis, and even sickle cell anemia. Just like vitamin B1, it is very helpful against Alzheimer's. Riboflavin is used and required for the proper development of many different parts of the body, including the skin, brain function, and blood cells.

11. Source of Vitamin D

This vitamin is responsible for helping with the absorption of calcium, magnesium, and phosphate. It also helps maintain strong bones. It follows that if you have low levels of vitamin D, then you will have weaker bones and muscle weakness, as well. And while vitamin D is found in very few foods, mushrooms happen to have a good amount, 1 IU in 18 grams of mushrooms, more than most foods.

12. Source of Vitamin B3

Niacin, also known as vitamin B3, is used to treat high cholesterol, so it is very helpful to reduce the risk of a heart attack and the narrowing of the heart arteries. Really, Niacin is good for the overall health of the body. It is good to have 16 milligrams of niacin a day, and most mushrooms have some of the best "vegetable" sources of niacin, giving 2.5 mg per cup (70 grams). Truly, mushrooms are wonderful for overall health.

13. Source of Vitamin B5

Pantothenic acid, also known as vitamin B5, is necessary for humans to take to metabolize the major macros; carbohydrates, fats, and proteins. While research has not definitely proven any of these, vitamin B5 has been used to treat a wide range of different problems, such as acne, autism, colitis, depression, nerve pain, gray hair, obesity, headaches, and even low blood sugar. This vitamin is essential for good overall health, and mushrooms are high in B5.

14. Source of Vitamin B6

Also known as Pyridoxine, this vitamin is used for many different reasons. This vitamin has been known to help treat mood and depression, improving levels of serotonin, dopamine, and other neurotransmitters. Like many other vitamins in mushrooms, vitamin B6 is known to help with reducing the risk of Alzheimer's disease and overall promoting brain health. It has also been known to reduce the symptoms of PMS, nausea during pregnancy, reduction of heart disease risk, help prevent cancer, and finally promoting overall eye health and preventing eye diseases. This is a super vitamin if there ever was one.

15. Source of Vitamin B9

Folate, also known as vitamin B9, is mainly taken by women who are planning to become pregnant or are pregnant presently. They help the body use fats and proteins, but not necessarily carbohydrates. There are no known risks in taking vitamin B9. If you have a lack of B9 in your system, you could start to experience forgetfulness, diarrhea, loss of appetite, or shortness of breath. Mushrooms are high in this vitamin and are used by pregnant women to support the growth of the fetus.

16. Source of Vitamin H

Biotin, also known as vitamin H, is very helpful in terms of metabolic processes, mostly in the utilization of fats, carbs, and proteins. So, vitamin H is used to break down these substances in the body for them to be used for energy. Mostly found in yeast, milk, and egg yolks, this is also found in small amounts in mushrooms. When combined with the many other health benefits of mushrooms, this is just a drop in the bucket.

17. Treatment of Skin Conditions

Skin conditions of all kinds are subject to be changed when you decide to consume mushrooms. Conditions such as eczema, acne, and even rosacea (which is the condition that results in small, pus-filled pimples on your wonderful face) can be treated by getting the right amounts of nutrients from mushrooms and extracts taken from mushrooms themselves.

18. Fighting against Aging

Kojic acid, which is also used to lighten the skin of people that eat mushrooms, is also useful as an antiaging unit in creams and lotions. Mushrooms are masters at changing the landscape of the face into what it was supposed to originally look like without any uneven skin tones, discoloration, or age spots. This is an unusual acid not found in many other places, so this is a wonderful reason to use and grow mushrooms.

19. Helps Treat Acne

Being high in Vitamin D, and we talked about why it is also so helpful later, mushrooms can help people with acne lesions. This is so helpful to the skin that some products use extracts from certain mushrooms to help treat skin conditions such as acne. This is a wonderful, natural solution to a natural problem for many people, as well as being a great alternative to other unnatural strategies.

20. Helps Lighten Skin

Not only do mushrooms help against acne and hydrating the skin, as we will talk about later, mushrooms also have a thing called kojic acid, which is known to be a natural skin lightening agent. This acid helps to prevent the production of melanin on the surface of your skin so that your skin has the ability to lighten up instead of darkening. This is helpful for those that have that goal in mind.

21. Hydration of Skin

Mushrooms are pumped full of this thing called hyaluronic acid, which acts as the body's moisturizer for your skin. Studies have shown that it reduces fine lines and wrinkles in the skin, as well as helping against the overall aging of the skin. This will cause the skin to look nice and smooth over time.

22. Destruction of Cancer Cells

The number of antioxidants in most edible mushrooms is a wonderful surprise to many new growers. Mushrooms have been proven to help with multiple types of cancers, including prostate, breast, lung, and many other types as well. Sources have been known to suggest that the vitamin, selenium, can prevent cancer, but there are no comprehensive studies to confirm this. Vitamin D and choline are also present in most known mushrooms, and these have been known to mitigate most forms of cancer, specifical choline.

23. Destruction of Viruses and Bacteria

This has been true with the flu virus as well as many other viruses throughout research terms. Paul Stamets and his team of researchers have done extensive work on this subject for further details. This was talked about in the introduction as well for more information.

24. Cleaning Polluted Soil

In a fascinating turn of events, mushrooms are grown in a pile of diesel sludge and trash bloom (if you could call what they do blooming). But their magic doesn't stop there. They start to allow for other grasses and small plants to start growing there, as well. Insects are attracted to the plants and mushrooms, the spores from the mushrooms continue to attract bugs, and then birds start to come. They drop seeds, and this continues the cycle until what was once a pile of crap is turned into a beautiful oasis of greenery and life. One last thing: the mushrooms can be eaten, and they are completely healthy, because of all the antioxidants in them. A truly amazing turn of events for the environment. Refer to point 41 for more information.

25. Restoration of Habitats by Polluting Factories

As we have seen with the research of Paul Stamets, regular mushrooms can transform wastelands into beautiful ecosystems. This information should also be found in the introduction.

26. Potential Source of Fuel?

This has not been proven to be completely effective yet, but there is research that suggests this would be an option in the near future.

27. Used Instead of Styrofoam

In several cases, mushrooms have been known to be able to be transformed into a different source of packing material that can replace Styrofoam. While this is still a new idea and is still a difficult thing to do at this point in its development, as time goes on it should become a better and better supplemental material for Styrofoam, and hopefully one day we will be able to replace Styrofoam completely and use mushroom fibers instead. The fibers are the part of the fungus found in the stem and could prove to be even more effective than conventional packing materials in the near future.

28. Killing Kings

Refer to the introduction for an explanation of this point. Not too good for Austria, but helpful to other European countries.

29. Promotion of Heart Health

Mushrooms are full of Vitamin C and Potassium, both of which are extremely healthy and helpful in overall heart health. And while it is helpful for people with type 2 diabetes such as in point 6, it is also helpful for those that do not have that problem. Studies have concluded that people with low vitamin C would have more cardiovascular problems and even cardiovascular disease. While vitamin C supplements have not been proven to help with these problems, dietary fiber is one of the helpful fibers in mushrooms, a fiber called beta-glucans has also been proven to lower cholesterol levels. Stems of mushrooms are full of these, so be sure to add these to your diet as an extra precaution

30. Boiling

This type of cooking the fungus will allow for most of the water in the mushroom to stay where it is, as well as kill any bacteria that were resting on the mushroom.

31. Frying

A few of the recipes found in the latter part of this chapter, and it is a favorite of most Americans.

32. Stir Fry

Since most mushrooms contain about 80% water, once they are put into a wok and fried up with rice, sauce, meat, and veggies, they make a wonderful addition to any diet. They are very easy to cook and have little to no preparation time. They are also a wonderful substitute for meat, as monks and other spirituals have used for hundreds of years for meat fasts.

33. Raw

This is probably the least safe way to eat mushrooms, but if you know what types of mushrooms are good to be eaten raw, then you should be completely fine.

34. Grilling

Although this will get rid of most of the minerals and water found in mushrooms, this will be an excellent choice, especially for mushrooms such as Portabellos.

35. Sauteing

A favorite for the finer culinary tastes among us, great for several of the recipes listed below.

36. Help Support Liver and Kidney Function in Your Pets

This was an interesting one me to see. I had no idea how mushrooms could be used for pets until I checked out this https://www.drbasko.com/portfolio-items/many-health-benefits-mushrooms-add-pets-diet.

37. Prevent Viral Infections in Your Pets

This point is also connected to the one above.

38. Contains Many Antioxidants

This is one of the best parts of the mushroom. There are so many of these in the average mushroom that one could get most of your daily needs of antioxidants in just a few cups of mushrooms a day. There are plenty of antioxidants found in mushrooms for the average person to utilize, and maybe someday, as more research comes out, be used as a medicine alongside modern medicine and research.

39. Garnish

Mushrooms are best served cut up into smaller pieces, and finding themselves in a salad for an added meaty kick is wonderful for any person who is going on a diet or is switching over to a vegetative diet more specifically.

40. Can produce Chitin

Mostly helpful as dietary fiber, mushrooms have certain elements that can be used to make Chitin, which is also a food thickening agent.

41. Turn Waste into Food

In a fascinating turn of events, mushrooms are grown in a pile of diesel sludge and trash bloom (if you could call what they do blooming). But their magic doesn't stop there. They start to allow for other grasses and small plants to start growing there, as well. Insects are attracted to the plants and mushrooms. The spores from the mushrooms continue to attract bugs, and then birds start to come. They drop seeds, and this continues the cycle until what was once a pile of crap is turned into a beautiful oasis of greenery and life. One last thing: the mushrooms can be eaten, and they are completely healthy, because of all the antioxidants in them.

42. Teeth Health

Multiple studies have shown that mushrooms can help clean teeth because of the minerals found in them, and extracts from mushrooms have also been found in certain types of toothpaste.

43. Making Beer, Wine, and Bread

Saccharomyces, also known as yeast, is completely necessary when it comes to making beer, wine, and bread. This is perhaps the most important reason fungi are used for over thousands of years of human development, albeit

MUSHROOMS

not the overall healthiest, but not specifically unhealthy at all. Without yeast, who knows what humankind would look like.

CHAPTER 6

FORAGING AND IDENTIFICATION

Overall, when it comes to identification, mushroom growers need to be careful in their selection of mushrooms and be ready to take extra precautions to be as safe as possible.

This book is primarily about mushroom growing and using, but this is also an important part of being a holistic mushroom lover.

There are a couple of old sayings when it comes to foraging for mushrooms:

"There are old mushroom foragers and bold mushroom foragers, However, there are no old, bold mushroom foragers."

"All hunters put life at risk, but for mushroomers, the moment of danger comes well after the quarry has been run to the ground...Finding the mushroom is the initiation, but eating it is the test." - John Thorne

Foraging for mushrooms has been a habitat of human beings in virtually every country for thousands of years at one point or another. Some cultures do so to find fungi to add to their otherwise weak diets, such as parts of Africa. Others, such as in Nepal, forage for mushrooms because of the money to be made, some foragers being able to make nearly half a year's salary during one growing season. Besides the economic reasons, there is also the fun of the act itself! In England, when schooling had become mandatory, teachers would let students go home early to explore the woods with their mothers to search for mushrooms for food as well as for a learning exercise.

As we have understood throughout this book, there are many ways to use mushrooms for health benefits and other reasons as well that we still don't have enough space to talk about. It serves one best to explore the benefits of them oneself. Mushrooms are wonderfully fun to search for on a cool autumn morning, and the thrill of the search is only added to the benefits given to the forager upon consuming the mushroom itself. This is considered better than cultivating your own mushrooms to some because of the thrill of the "quiet hunt" (as coined by Antonio Carluccio in his book *The Complete Mushroom Book* in 2003)

Jean-Jacques Paulet made the first useful guide in the 1790s to assist the flourish of new foragers looking for adventure in the woodlands of France. Since then, we have advanced in many ways in the expansion of learning how to identify mushrooms better. I would suggest getting a good guidebook that is sufficient for the area you hope to be foraging in. This will take a lot of grief off of you and make you feel safer in your foraging, which should be more of an enjoyable activity.

Here is a list of questions you should ask when you find a mushroom in the field and are not sure about its origin or its name:

- Where is it growing?
- How is it growing?
- Is it growing in a cluster?
- Is it growing by itself?
- What color is its cap, gills, base, etc.?
- Is the base straight, or is it bulbous?
- Does it have a sac?
- What does the mushroom feel like?
- What does it smell like?

There are not many tools that a forager needs in their collection. The most important tool you can have is a magnifying glass and a knife, the magnifying glass for helping to identify certain characteristics of the mushroom, and the nice for cutting stems. Other tools that are necessary for foraging are some sort of tool to dig with a basket for keeping all the different species separate, rubber boots, etc. Some forgers find that using something called a Spore bag works very well to prevent any damaging to the artist that they have; this will also get rid of any creatures that want to come home with you in the mushroom caps. As there are also rules for identification, you should always check out the size, the color, the gill connectivity, the cross-section, bruising color, odor spore print, and environments of the mushroom before being absolutely certain of its original name.

A few things to keep in mind when looking for those tasty edibles in your next quiet hunt for mushrooms. *Only eat mushrooms that you are completely sure about.* You need to learn about both edible mushrooms as well as poisonous mushrooms to tell them apart from each other. Take the time to study your guide for a good amount of both edible and poisonous mushrooms to be as safe as possible on your next adventure. Next, *don't be hasty in your selection and take your time.* You need to pick the **entire** mushroom to make a positive identification. The base of the mushroom needs to be shown for a good identification to be made. The second thing to do with this mushroom, if you are not absolutely sure about the nature of the mushroom, is to take a spore print, especially with grilled mushrooms. Next, *eat only a small bit of the mushroom at first to make sure you are not adversely affected by the mushroom.* Even if the mushroom is not poisonous to most people, it may be disagreeable with you and your body. It is better to be safe rather than sorry.

CHAPTER 7
THE POWER OF A MEDICINAL MUSHROOM

Mushrooms are one of the most nutrient-dense foods in the world, providing the bacteria in our gut with unique types of fiber not found in any other foods. Recently, a new trend has kicked off, discussions about medicinal mushrooms, the power they have and what they can do for us.

A medicinal mushroom is a subcategory that, as well as having a great taste and plenty of nutrients, is also packed with proven medicinal benefits. The big question is, do they live up to the hype? In short, yes, they do, and that is what we're going to be talking about in this chapter.

Medicinal mushrooms have long been used in traditional medicine for centuries and across many different cultures. In contrast to many of the other alternative medicine products and techniques, medicinal mushrooms are the subject of hundreds of studies and have long been validated as having beneficial effects. Somewhere along the line, I'm sure you heard that your immune system could benefit from medicinal mushrooms, but was you also aware that they provide great benefits for the cardiovascular system, your blood sugar, endocrine system, and so much more? They can even help you to fight fatigue!

Before we dive into all that, though, we need to take a quick look at the basics.

What is a Medicinal Mushroom?

You already know that a mushroom is the fruit body of different species of fungus. Fungi have their own kingdom and are an important organism that plays a vital role in every ecosystem. Specifically, they contribute to the decay of animal and plant matter, as well as recycling it. Mushrooms have long been studied for the compounds that make up their unique ability to digest and recycle other organisms.

So, why are medicinal mushrooms so-called? Because there have been many studies on their abilities to sustain and improve life. At current, there are about 700 species deemed to have the right properties to be called medicinal. That said, not every one of those species is backed up by scientific studies, at least not yet.

However, there are some very well-known species long used in traditional cultures, particularly Asian cultures, but also in parts of Africa and Eastern Europe; these mushrooms do have the scientific backing and include:

- Chaga (*Inonotus obliquus*)

- Cordyceps (*Cordyceps Sinensis*)
- Lion's Mane (*Hericium Erinaceus*)
- Reishi (*Ganoderma lucidum*)
- Shiitake (*Lentinus edodes*)
- Turkey Tail (*Trametes Versicolor*)

This is just a tiny example of the more than 14,000 mushroom species and up to 10 million fungi species around the world, so what has been studied is the tip of the iceberg, so to speak.

Physiological Effects of a Medicinal Mushroom

Medicinal mushrooms come with many benefits, lots of them physiological, and we're going to look at the ways they can benefit our health. All of these are backed up by years of scientific studies.

The Immune System

The immune system is the most well-known mechanism backing up the effects of these mushrooms, and most of us will have read some news stories about the immunomodulating and anti-tumor effects of medicinal mushrooms. But there's more to it than that.

There are other physiological actions identified over the years, demonstrating just how potent these mushrooms are on the immune system.

Antitumor – more than 30 types of medicinal mushrooms contain polysaccharides that have been proven to help prevent tumors from forming. They also exhibit direct activity against tumors and can also stop metastasis, which is when cancer spreads from the originating organ to one or more other organs or locations in the body. More specifically, scientific research shows that those effects are even stronger when they are used together with chemotherapy, and both can be used safely at the same time. T cells modulate the activity, so the person's thymus and T cell system need to be intact.

Immunomodulating – Some medicinal mushrooms contain components that can induce a genetic expression. This then leads to several immunomodulatory cytokine receptors and cytokines being created, allowing the immune system to provide the right response to stressors and damping down unwanted inflammation.

Antioxidants and Free Radical Scavengers - these scavengers are compounds that can neutralize both oxidized compounds and free radicals in the human body. Antioxidants also go to work in the liver enzymes vita for elimination and detoxification. Some medicinal mushroom compounds have also been discovered to have an incredibly potent capacity in terms of antioxidants, and this most certainly plays a part in both anti0inflammatory and antitumor properties.

Antifungal, Antiparasitic, and Antibacterial – there are now studies that make comparisons between the antimicrobial activities in medicinal mushrooms with those of antibiotics produced by the pharmaceutical industry. Right now, it is thought that to stay vital out in nature, mushrooms need antimicrobial properties, and, when we consume the mushrooms, we also get some of those benefits. What is interesting is that some studies now show shiitake mushrooms to be antimicrobial agents fighting infections that are often resistant to treatment, such as E.coli 0157:H7, and shigella.

Anti-Inflammatory – while some of the categories discussed above already count as being anti-inflammatory but it's worth highlighting that medicinal mushrooms, in general, are considered to have excellent anti-inflammatory properties. Some of the polysaccharides have been shown to exhibit anti-inflammatory activity, including phenols, terpenoids, and proteoglycans.

It's worth diverting our attention for a moment to look at what this could mean for the way autoimmune diseases are managed and looking at a few of the concepts in detail. Mushrooms contain a fibrous component called beta-glucans, and these have the potential to be bioactive. The beta-glucans are tiny molecules and can easily bind directly to immune cells. Because of that, they affect immune activity, together with the indirect effects of the gut microbiome.

It was this that was responsible for the rationale behind the avoidance of using medicinal mushrooms or their extracts on the AIP – the autoimmune protocol. Anyone who suffers from an autoimmune disease must be very wary of anything that may have a stimulating effect on their immune system but, in recent times, more studies have been done. These now show that medicinal mushrooms are not immunostimulatory; instead, they are immunomodulatory, which means they rebalance an immune system that is out of kilter. One of the best-studied mushrooms in this area is the reishi mushroom.

Studies done on patients with rheumatoid arthritis showed a decrease in joint pain alongside a reduction in interleukin(IL)-18 – this has a potent activation effect on TH1 cells, and the same studies showed that cytokines, like measured inflammatory cells, did not increase. Another study of lupus in mice showed that a supplement containing reishi extract brought about a decrease in autoantibodies and an increase in survival rates.

Yet another lupus mouse study demonstrated that reishi increased the regulatory T cell ratio to both TH1 and TH17 cells, alongside cytokine changes, such as Il-10, IL-17, and IL-21 decreases and IL2, and IL-12P70 increases.

Lastly, a mouse model based on Alzheimer's disease demonstrated gene expression changes correlating to a decrease in the activity of the disease, thanks to supplementation with reishi. What is truly fascinating is that the reishi extract has also been shown to help in cancer, increasing the T cell (cytotoxic) activity, as well as having an effect on angiogenesis and the growth of cancer cells.

All of this paints a picture of extracts of medicinal mushrooms, in particular, reishi, having huge benefits where the immune system is under-active, for example, when you have the flu or a common cold; they are also beneficial in cases of overactive function, such as the many autoimmune diseases and in fighting cancer and stopping it from metastasizing.

The Autoimmune Protocol does include whole mushrooms, such as the shiitake, but there is a clear need for more confirmatory research before extracts may be given a definitive go-ahead for those with autoimmune diseases. For now, it's probably best to avoid them

The Cardiovascular System

Medicinal mushrooms have also been shown to be beneficial to the cardiovascular system. As it is with the immune system, studies have been done, showing they help in combatting some diseases while providing preventative benefits at the same time. Some species are proven to assist in the treatment of ischemic heart disease, the commonest cause of a heart attack, of chronic heart failure, and arrhythmia. It is the anti-inflammatory benefits of medicinal mushrooms that increase the dilation in the blood vessels and increases the blood circulation to the heart. And it works the same way for circulation to the brain too.

It has also been shown that medicinal mushroom supplementation can lower LDL cholesterol, total cholesterol, and inhibit the time taken for platelet aggregation, which prevents plaque. All of this works towards preventing heart disease, and one of the best-known mushrooms for this is the cordyceps.

The Respiratory System

Clinical trials have been done on some medicinal mushrooms and their properties in improving lung health, as well as traditional usage for some lung conditions. The cordyceps mushroom, for example, has long been used as a form of treatment for asthma, bronchitis, and other respiratory disorders. Many studies have been done on patients who have asthma, and the effectiveness of the mushroom was proven after the usage for a period of five to six weeks. Another study looked at how cordyceps affected patients who had stages I, II, and III non-small cell lung cancer, and showed it was beneficial.

The Endocrine System

Blood sugar regulation is one of the most studied benefits on health that medicinal mushrooms have. The mushrooms contain fantastic prebiotics, required for the gut microbiome, and providing support for a healthy gut. Gut health is an important factor in blood sugar regulation – it isn't all about carbohydrate and sugar consumption, however, to get the best benefits, you need to consume whole mushrooms and/or whole mushrooms in powdered form. With that, you get the full impact of the unique fibers in mushrooms, called chitin, and the nutrients.

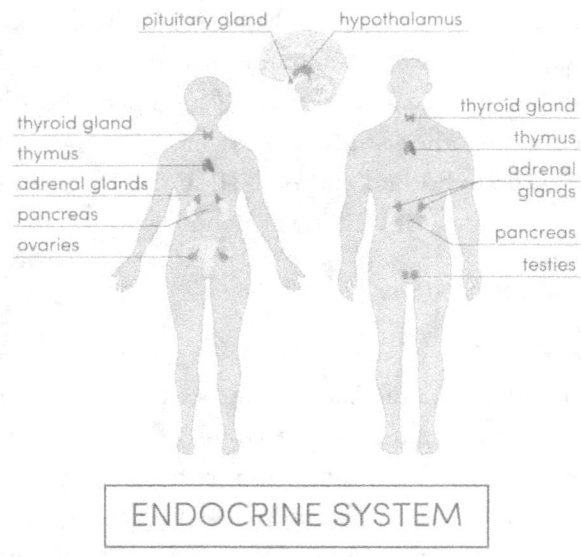

ENDOCRINE SYSTEM

Elimination and Detoxification

That covers your liver, kidneys, and your gut health. China has long used the mushroom for its benefits in treating kidney failure, chronic nephritis, and other kidney diseases. Medicinal mushrooms have been studied for their links to water balance, and this, of course, can help with kidney disease. By the same token, because they are such strong antioxidants, the medicinal mushroom is fantastic or the liver too. In short, their strong antioxidant support means that the liver doesn't have to do so much work in generating them to detoxify the cells and eliminate toxic substances.

As mentioned earlier, mushrooms contain chitin, which is a unique fiber. More importantly, it is a fermentable oligosaccharide fiber. It is comprised of long chains containing N-acetylglucosamine, which is a glucose derivative that has amino acids attached to it. We can only get this from fungi, such as medicinal mushrooms, shellfish scales, fish scales, and insect exoskeletons. As it happens, chitin is a powerful prebiotic and studies show that it helps different gut-friendly bacteria, such as Lactobacillus, Bifidobacterium, Bacteroides, and Akkermansia. At the same time, it reduces the level of Desulfovibrio, which is an inflammatory microbe commonly found in those who suffer from inflammatory bowel disease. Mice studies show that the oligosaccharides, produced when chitin is digested, modulate microbiota in the gut to fight against metabolic syndrome, induced by diet, and slowing down the rate at which the gut barrier is destroyed.

Chitosan, another fiber made up of the same molecules, also contains D-glucosamine molecules, distributed randomly throughout the chain. This is only found naturally in the cell walls o mushrooms and other fungi. Mice studies showed that it increased the diversity of gut microbes, increased levels of Bacteroides, and decreased levels of firmicute and Shigella and Escherichia, both pathogenic genera. Where the mice were diabetic, chitosan reshaped the microbiota in a bid to produce an effect that was anti0diabetic.

So, it would seem that, to keep your gut in tip-top shape, you should be eating medicinal mushrooms, whole and as natural as they grow.

General Wellbeing and Fatigue

While this isn't all that easy to measure fully in research and studies, it is an important one to include. The primary reason for that is that it is one of the most traditional and well-known uses of the medicinal mushroom. Studies show that those who regularly consume the mushrooms say they don't suffer from fatigue or exhaustion as much. The same studies on animals showed that the mushrooms promote an increase in oxygen availability to tissues and increase ATP production, the molecule used for energy in the cells.

By the same token, studies on medicinal mushrooms for supporting chemotherapy show that the side effects of the treatment are reduced when medicinal mushrooms are used alongside it.

Whole Medicinal Mushrooms or Extracts?
Right now, you can buy any number of products that contain medicinal mushrooms, and it is clear that the hype is correct. The thing is, although you can buy any product that contains the mushrooms, there are some products that are better than others – those that have the correct mushroom sourcing and extraction methods. Most of the scientific research focuses on two main extraction methods – hot water and hot water with alcohol. These

methods both mimic the modern and traditional Chinese methods of preparing medicinal mushrooms.

Traditionally, decoctions have been used to prepare medicinal mushrooms; a decoction is much like a "super tea"; the mushrooms are placed in boiling water and simmered for between 20 minutes and two hours. Doing this helps to break the cellular walls of tough mushrooms, allowing the components into the water. One of those components is chitin, the main component of the fungi's cell walls. Using hot water to extract the components, with alcohol or without, is the only proper way of breaking the cell walls down and extracting the chitin that is so beneficial to the gut microbiome. And some mushrooms provide more chitin in this way than you get eating the whole mushroom.

Some products contain whole ground mushrooms. While eating whole mushrooms is recommended, the ground format isn't the subject of many studies. Where you can purchase medicinal mushrooms whole, such as the shiitake mushroom, you should add them to your food when you cook; for others, use the hot water methods for maximum benefits.

One more thing you should look out for are those extracts that are made from the whole mushroom and not just the mycelium. This is normally grown in a grain medium, and products with mycelium may well be misleading – most of the fiber is from the grain the mycelium is grown in and not from the mushrooms, which means it isn't all that beneficial. Look on the label for the beta-glucan measurement and, if there, the triterpenoid content, as well as looking for those products that have gluten-free certification.

Overall, the medicinal mushrooms do live up to their hype, and we should all be adding them, in some form or another, to our daily diets.

Six Medicinal Mushrooms to Boost your Health

For thousands of years, medicinal mushrooms have been a big part of Eastern medicine and, these days, they are growing in popularity for mainstream use. Typically, they are taken in powder form, as very few can be eaten raw or whole, medicinal mushrooms can be found in all forms. One of the best ways to get your fix is to add a spoonful of powder to whatever you are eating or drinking.

The health benefits provided by medicinal mushrooms are endless, but every mushroom is different, and each one has its own unique advantages in terms of health benefits. Do keep in mind that they are not a cure-all though and are still relatively new in Western medicine. While much research has already been done, more is needed so, for now, think of them as an addition, a helping hand in combatting stress, for boosting your immune system and fighting cancer or inflammatory diseases.

Some are better than others for certain conditions, so let's look at six medicinal mushrooms and what they can do for you.

Reishi Mushrooms Soften the Edge

Reishi is the fungi version of Xanax and is one of the more popular of the medicinal mushrooms. And there is an excellent reason for that – reishi can do so much. It helps with weight loss, ensures your immune system is working as it should be, and can even put up a fierce fight against cancer cells.

However, it's most unique property is that it is a claiming mushroom. That is down to triterpene, a compound this mushroom has in spades. Triterpene is a mood-booster, and it can help to ease depression, alleviate anxiety, help you sleep better, and more. But it doesn't stop there, Reishi also helps promote healing, and it can sharpen up your focus too.

Try using a spoonful to make a cup of healing, hot tea, or even stir it into a chocolate pudding.

Boost Your Brain with Lion's Mane

If your brain is foggy, a spot of lion's mane can clear things up for you. A 'pom-pom' mushroom is a feathery fungus full of antioxidants that can help strengthen your immune system in the way most medicinal mushrooms can. This is a rare mushroom, though, because it promotes the growth of NGF (nerve growth factor) called bioprotein, along with myelin, which is what insulates nerve fibers.

Both myelin and NFG are critical to the health of our brains; if they are not balanced, we are more at risk of neurological diseases, such as multiple sclerosis or Alzheimer's disease. Studies have also shown the lion's main mushroom helps improve cognition, alleviate irritability, anxiety, and increase concentration levels.

Add a spoon of lion's mane to yerba tea to provide a drink packed with antioxidants that clear your mind.

Use Chaga to Boost Your Antioxidants
Chaga mushrooms are one of the medicinal mushroom powerhouses, packed with antioxidants that help fight inflammation and free radicals. It is a dark black in color and helps fight against oxidative stress, which causes aging of the skin. It can also help to slow down or even prevent cancer growth, and studies have shown it lowers LDL cholesterol. Most of the research on the change mushroom has been done on mice, and human cells, and all the signs point to it being a fantastic mushroom for your health, inside your body and out.

Add a spoon of powder to a smoothie or add it to a chai latte.

MUSHROOMS

Chaga Mushroom (see above)

Keep Your Heart Healthy With Shiitake

If you are already using shiitake mushrooms in your cooking, then good for you, but the benefits of this popular mushroom go far beyond taste.

Shiitake mushrooms are excellent for the heart and have been proven to lower LDL cholesterol. Some of their compounds inhibit the absorption of cholesterol in the liver and well as inhibiting its growth. They are also a rich source of phytonutrients, useful for stopping plaque from building up and, following studies on rats also shown to keep blood circulation and blood pressure healthy

Add a spoonful of powder to any recipe to give it a healthy, hearty boost of goodness.

Use Turkey Tail to Fight Cancer

Practically all medicinal mushrooms contain cancer-fighting properties, thanks primarily to the high level of antioxidants they contain. However, the turkey tail mushroom takes things further.

It has a compound called PSK, or polysaccharide-K. This compound is excellent at providing the immune system with stimulation and is so effective that, in Japan, it is now an approved prescription drug to fight cancer. Studies on the turkey tail mushroom show that it improves survival rates for certain cancers, can fight against leukemia and helps boost the immune systems of those undergoing chemotherapy. It is important, however, that you do NOT stop taking prescribed drugs without speaking to your doctor first.

Try adding a spoonful to a smoothie to give it an immune-boosting punch or even have a go at making a batch of turkey tail ale!

Cordyceps Is The Perfect Pick-Me-Up

If you feel like your energy is flagging or you need a boost before you work out, reach for the cordyceps. This is one of the best-known mushrooms to provide stimulation, and not just for energy levels, either – it also works on the libido!

Cordyceps is excellent at supporting efficient oxygen utilization in the body and ensuring efficient blood flow. This is one of the most helpful mushrooms or people who work out a lot, and for athletes and studies show it doesn't just improve performance, it also helps to speed up muscle recovery after working out.

Add a spoonful to your pre-workout meal for an energy boost and your post-workout meal to help hasten recovery.

The Takeaway

One of the best ways of getting the fantastic benefits from these mushrooms is to add a spoonful to your meals or drinks every day. Don't take any more than one or two tablespoons per day, though – even if you do feel much better afterward, taking more won't make a difference, and as most of these mushrooms are still under trial for their benefits its best to wait and see before you take more.

Do make sure you consult your doctor before taking any of these; you need to be sure that it is safe for you to add them, particularly if you are pregnant, nursing, or taking any other medications. Make sure you do your homework too – like anything, some mushrooms can cause allergies, stomach upsets, and other side effects.

CHAPTER 8

COMMON MISTAKES TO AVOID WHEN GROWING MUSHROOMS

Provided you follow the right steps, cultivating mushrooms is a relatively straightforward process, and you can reap the rewards for many years to come. However, it's a fact of life that things go wrong, and failures happen. It could be down to sheer bad luck, contamination, even environmental issues but, whatever causes your crop to fail, you need to step back and work out what's gone wrong.

When you troubleshoot a poor or failed crop, first look at the technique you used. It may be that you did something wrong, or it wasn't the right techniques for the particular mushroom you are trying to grow. After that, you can look at everything else. Be thorough and eliminate obvious and/or potential problems. Be careful, though; sometimes, when you fix what you think is a problem, you can make another problem worse.

Sometimes, even discovering a problem can't fix it – it might be too late to save things. Learn from it and get the next crop right. You can follow these tips to help you be more prepared:

The Problem – The Medium is Inoculated, but No Fruit is Produced

If the medium is inoculated correctly but doesn't produce any mushrooms, the first solution is simple – time. It can take more than a year for some mushroom strains to produce, and that means you need a lot of patience – something many beginners are short of. The answer is to stagger your mushroom cultivation over two or three years, and you should have a regular harvest.

That said, there are things you can do to get things moving a bit faster or give the mycelium a boost if it appears to be too slow in fruiting. The first thing is moisture. Make sure the growing medium you use, be it wood chips, logs, whatever, is misted a minimum of once per week, more in warmer, dryer times. You can also soak logs for 24 hours in cold water.

The next thing is to ensure there is sufficient airflow. Place logs outside in areas that have plenty of ventilation, with air coming from all directions, or as many as possible, anyway.

If you are cultivating mushrooms indoors, keep the windows open, or a fan switched on to keep the air flowing through the room. Although you don't need to, it might be helpful to moisten the medium and the spawn before inoculation and, immediately after inoculation, moisten the medium again, to stop the spawn drying and to hasten things.

Contaminated spawn is a problem, too, but you can avoid this by making sure you handle it carefully. Thoroughly wash your hands before you handle it, and when you take a break from inoculating the medium. Never allow the spawn to come into contact with any surface other than the medium you are using and, if you are ill, definitely do not handle the spawn. The human body plays host to many different types of bacteria, as does the environment, and all of these have the potential for contaminating the spawn, taking hold before the mycelium can become dominant.

If you can, pasteurize the medium before you inoculate it. Typically, this is only done when you use a straw. It should be heated just enough to get rid of the harmful bacteria but retain the beneficial bacteria. If you use a sterilization process, with very high heat levels, pressure, or chemicals, you will kill all the bacteria, including the good stuff, and that leaves the medium wide-open for the bad stuff to creep in again. The ideal temperature for pasteurization is 160°F to 180°F. To do it, heat water to between 160°F and 170°F and then leave the straw to soak for an hour – do maintain the temperature throughout.

Problem – The Mycelium is Growing, but there is No Fruit

If you find, when you look at your growing medium, that there are fibrous, white materials, the mycelium is growing.

However, depending on the type of mushroom you are cultivating, you may have to wait a while for the fruit to appear. If you don't see any for some time after or they do start growing but then abort, there could be any number of reasons. First, you may have used the wrong match of medium and strain, or you could be using a bad strain. In the latter case, next time, choose a different strain and, in the former, do some meticulous research on what medium goes with the strain you are trying to grow. What you mustn't do, if you see tiny pins or mushrooms, is assume they have aborted - often, these will appear long before full growth is achieved.

Problem – The Substrate Doesn't Produce

Make sure you thoroughly understand the correct region for each strain, along with the growth cycle, before you decide that there is a problem. There are three primary designations for growth conditions – warm, cold, or wide-range weather. Each indicates when the strain will fruit, not the type of growing conditions. In other words, if your region is moderately temperate, all three strains could be planted, so you get a staggered harvest.

The wide-range strains tend to fruit in early spring, midsummer or late all, depending on whether your climate is southerly or northerly. The cold strains produce late fall and early spring in a northerly region and, in the southerly regions, throughout most of the winter months. And the warm strains tend to produce midsummer right through to early all in most regions.

MUSHROOMS

Problem – The Mushrooms are Deformed

If you get overlong stems, caps that are cracked or underdeveloped, and other types of deformity, it may be that you don't have enough light, insufficient airflow, or too much moisture. Most mushroom strains require a level of diffused light for proper growth because, like most plants, mushrooms move towards the light when they grow.

If there isn't enough light, the stem will grow tall and spindly as it tries to push the cap towards the light; the result will also be a thin, narrow, and small cap. Too much or too little moisture may also result in problems. Never allow logs to stand in water or leave any medium in a place that is always moist. A certain amount of moisture is needed, but it must be allowed to evaporate. Too little and the mushrooms will be brittle, dry, and have cracked caps. If this starts to happen, add some more moisture consistently. And the airflow is also a requirement, as a high level of CO^2 helps to prevent the 'fuzzy feet' mushrooms develop when there isn't enough fresh air.

Problem – Mushrooms Spoil Very Quickly After Harvesting

If you harvest your mushrooms late, they can spoil. Don't harvest late or, if it cannot be avoided, use the mushrooms quickly. The best time to harvest is when the mushroom cap is dry and turned down. Try not to harvest when the mushrooms are wet.

MUSHROOMS

If you are growing mushrooms for packaging and selling at a market, chill them before you package them and use breathable containers with cellophane covering.

You may come across other problems when you cultivate mushrooms, but these are the most likely ones. If you follow the steps carefully, you shouldn't run into any trouble. Make sure you do your research thoroughly before you start, making sure you use the correct medium and are growing in the right environment. Patience is key – time is a massive factor in mushroom cultivation> all you need to do is get things going, and then sit back and wait, monitoring your crop carefully of course.

BONUS CHAPTER

GROWING GOURMET MUSHROOMS FOR PROFIT – FAQ

Shiitake mushrooms, oysters, and other gourmet mushrooms are a joy to grow, especially if you have a decent market for selling them. Traditionally, they are grown outside on logs and can still be found in a lot of different areas. Now, though, you can grow them in bags indoors, using sawdust or straw as a growing medium.

Interested in making a pile of mushroom gold? These are the answers to the common questions about gourmet mushrooms:

1. **Why would you consider gourmet mushrooms?**

For two great reasons. First, when you grow them indoors, you can control the environment – the humidity, light, and temperature – to ensure you get the best possible crop. You get a bigger harvest, and that leads to more profit than you would get from traditional crops grown on logs. Second, you can get up to six crops every year from the same amount of space – more steady income.

2. **Can gourmet mushrooms be grown in my area?**

Because shiitake and oyster mushrooms will grow indoors, you can grow them whatever area you live in – you are not dependent on the outside climate. A shed will do the trick, a greenhouse, a barn even a spare room or basement can be used for growing.

3. Which mushrooms are the best?

Shiitake and oyster mushrooms are popular and easy to sell, simply because the market is already there. Stick with these, and you'll make your money. Yes, you could grow other exotics, but most need more skill than these two, and you might find it tougher to get your market.

4. How do you propagate gourmet mushrooms?

Because mushrooms belong to the fungi family, they produce spores, not seeds. Generally, the spores are cultivated on rye grain; when the grain has been 'colonized' by the growing plant, it is then used for inoculating the growing substrate or medium, usually sawdust from hardwood or straw. After inoculation, the mushrooms will spread, and we get the fruit – the mushrooms. Try it – it is a fantastic process to watch.

5. If I only grow mushrooms part-time, can I make any money?

Absolutely! Mushrooms don't take much space – a small area can produce large harvests. It is one of the best cash crops for people who don't have the land the time or even the inclination to grow large-scale, conventional crops. It only takes a couple of minutes every day to check on your bags of inoculated substrate. Most gourmet growers do it as a part-time job, working at their 'real' jobs the rest of the time.

6. Can I use compost to grow shiitake and oyster mushrooms?

You can, but it isn't the best medium, and it may cause issues leading to a smaller harvest. Most growers used sterilized substrates and grow indoors; that way, spores from wild mushrooms can't cause contamination. When your mushrooms have almost finished fruiting, and you chuck the substrate you used on the compost pile, you may get more, but it will only be a small yield.

7. When do I harvest the mushrooms?

Commercial growth of shiitake and oyster mushrooms is done indoors, where humidity, light, and temperature are controlled to ensure fast growth. When mushrooms appear, they come in what is known as 'flushes,' and you can expect the first one to be the largest – that's when it's time to bring in the first harvest. After that, there will be a few more flushes, but there won't be so many mushrooms – a lot f commercial growers tend to harvest only the first flush.

8. Where can I sell gourmet mushrooms?

The mushrooms are at their best when they are first picked, so most tend to be sold locally. Many growers sell to local restaurants, co-ops, foo stores and straight to customers at farmer's markets. Gourmet mushrooms don't ship to well, so its best to sell them fresh, locally. This also means you won't be competing with the commercial suppliers from out of state, and your customers know they are getting the freshest mushrooms.

9. Can I make anything from the mushrooms?

Yes. some of the most popular products are pickled mushrooms, dehydrated mushrooms, mushroom jerky (great for vegetarians), mushroom seasonings, and even your own growing kits.

10. Do these mushrooms have better nutritional value than standard mushrooms?

Studies show that shiitake and oyster mushrooms are high in nutrition and are medicinal in nature. They contain high levels of antioxidants to help protect your cells, of potassium, zinc, vitamin C, calcium, vitamin B, vitamin B2, and niacin. Shiitake mushrooms have also been shown to provide antiviral support, help lower cholesterol and support the cardiovascular system, as well as having immune-boosting properties and potential anticancer properties.

11. How much money can I make selling gourmet mushrooms?

The mushroom crop cycle is quite short, around six weeks, so in a small space, you can make a reasonably steady income. If you grow in bags indoors, you can produce around 25 pounds of mushrooms per square foot. Let's see what that translates to. We'll assume you are growing your mushrooms in a shed, 12 feet by 12 feet; that gives you a growing area of 144 square feet, and that could give you a yearly yield of 3600 pounds of mushrooms. Let's say the price is $12 per pound – half your crop is sold at that price and the rest at $6 per pound – that will get you a little more than $32,000 per year. Your expenses won't be too much – that's a pretty healthy income for a part-time job!

12. How much money do I need to start a business?

You don't need to splash out on tons of pricey equipment here, so the costs can be quite cheap, no more than a couple of hundred dollars. You will need the LED fluorescent lights, dirt cheap to buy and run, so your electricity bill won't even be noticeably affected – unless you are growing acres of mushrooms!

By being able to grow these mushrooms inside, it doesn't matter where you are located and how much or little space you have available. You don't have to worry about the weather as you control the conditions, so really, the time is ripe for you to start your gourmet mushroom growing business now.

MUSHROOMS

CONCLUSION

What more is there to say about mushrooms? Much, but for our purposes, we will conclude the book here. But there are a few things that I want to bring up before we end the book completely. There are many resources out there that will aid your experience with mushrooms, and many of these resources I have used throughout this book, so hopefully, these resources I give you will be of assistance to you in the near future:

Mushroom by Nicholas Money: This was a helpful resource for me when I was first starting out with my research. Nicholas discusses the overall political-ness of mushrooms and how they have changed the world as a whole, before moving on to more complex ideas I couldn't clearly comprehend. A good study for anyone with love for mushrooms.

Mushroom: A Global History by Cynthia Bertelsen: This was a terrific book, and the thoughts of Cynthia inspired much of the information found in this book. She clearly lays out the idea of mycophobia and mycophilia, namely the fear of mushrooms and the love of mushrooms. She is a wonderfully credible source, and I am glad to have found her early on in my research for this book, as she has led me through many discussions and interviews with friends and families on the subject of mushrooms. This is a wonderful introduction to mushrooms for anyone interested. A quick and easy read packed full of information

Alfie Aesthetics: No discussion of mushrooms is complete without talking about this semi-professional forager and mushroom hunter. He has a wonderful YouTube channel of 287K subscribers (his content deserves thousands more) and has plenty of different videos talking about his adventures in the woods looking for different edible and useful mushrooms. He does a lot of different videos dedicated to survival and entertaining commentaries on his experiences in the woods, so whatever you are looking for, I would suggest Alfie. One comment suggested that he has the knowledge of a college professor, the identification skills of a mycologist, and the humor of a drunk pervert, and I have got to say that is Alfie to a T. If that sounds appealing to you, PLEASE check this guy out. I wouldn't have wanted to write this book without his knowledge and enthusiasm for mushrooms and other fungi.

ID books: This is one of the helpful books you can look into getting once you get more and more serious on foraging for mushrooms. There are hundreds of other books you can look into, just make sure to get one that you can use in your own country and is up to date with all the best information and research. This book specifically helped me with research for random facts about mushrooms that helped with the overall flow of the book, so for a helpful book on identification and helpful facts as well, I would recommend this one for sure.

MUSHROOMS

You have heard of all the benefits of mushrooms and such, whether they be health benefits or otherwise, and I hope this has given you some direction in which you want to start trying out mushrooms more in the near future. Here, I will review the information placed throughout the book in a manner that will allow you to go back and reference the information you are looking for in a quick way.

MUSHROOM FACTS

Common mushrooms to grow: Maitake, Enoki, Oyster, Shiitake, Lions Mane, and Wine Cap.

One quick step you need to follow in order to grow a mushroom: get the right substrate and container, steam pasteurization, incubation, and harvest.

There are several parts of mushrooms: spores, stem, gill, mycelium, hypha, volva, and the cap.

The life cycle of a mushroom is as follows: Inoculation, Spore Germination, Mycelial Expansion, Hyphal Knot, Primordia Formation, Fruitbody Selection, Mature Fruitbody, and Spore Release.

There are many wild, edible mushrooms out there on the North American continent, and it would serve you well to take the time to learn how to ID them. These include but are not limited to: The Field Mushroom, Caesar Mushroom, Honey Mushroom, Wood Ears, Giant Puffballs, Common Chanterelle, Smooth Chanterelle, Black Trumpets, Brick Tops, Lobster Mushrooms, Pear-Shaped Puffballs, The Parasol, Oysters, and Cauliflower Mushrooms.

There are seven categories of mushrooms: Cultivated Mushrooms, Wild Mushrooms, Medical Mushrooms, Psychoactive Mushrooms, Edible Mushrooms, Poisonous Mushrooms, Useful Mushrooms (For Other Reasons)

MUSHROOM CULTIVATION

A Step-by-Step Guide to Growing Gourmet Mushrooms at Home and Finding Fungi

By Tom Gordon

INTRODUCTION

When it comes to farming, there is one crop that is often overlooked: Mushrooms. This particular type of fungi doesn't come up in conversations about farming very often, but they really should. They're a little weird to grow, especially if you don't know anything about mushrooms or fungi, as they aren't planted in the ground like potatoes or carrots. But they can be an incredibly profitable crop, and they are actually easier to grow indoors rather than outdoors. That makes them a wonderful choice for those that live in an apartment. You might not have the space to set up a hydroponic system to grow large vegetable crops, but you can grow a crop of mushrooms with barely any room at all.

In the volume you hold in your hands, we're going to be getting to know these fascinating growths. Chapter One will look at the reasons why you should become involved in raising your own mushrooms. These range from the variety of tastes to the money they can make you and more. From there, we'll move to Chapter Two and an overview of the mushroom cultivation process that we'll be exploring throughout the book. Chapter Three will examine the different types of mushrooms that you may want to grow, ranging from portobello mushrooms to enoki mushrooms, and a whole lot more.

Once you have an idea of what you want to grow, it will

be time to turn to Chapter Four, where you'll learn how to prepare your grow room. Chapter Five lays out the different methods that you can use for growing, and Chapter Six begins the process of growing itself. Once we have grown our mushrooms, we'll want to preserve them so that they last longer. We cover this in Chapter Seven.

Chapter Eight shifts the focus from mushrooms to look at fungi as a whole so that you understand the different types, how it reproduces, and where you can find it. Chapter Nine turns back to mushrooms to look at how you can earn money from your crop. We close out finally with a few delicious recipes for ways to enjoy your freshly grown mushrooms.

By the end of this book, you'll have everything you need to start growing mushrooms to eat, to sell, and to share with your friends. You might find it a little bit confusing in the beginning, but this is only because mushrooms have a unique way of growing that makes them stand out from the other vegetable crops. But if you stick with it, everything will become clear, and you'll have the knowledge necessary to raise some delicious mushrooms in the comfort of your own home.

CHAPTER 1

BEST OF MUSHROOMS

You might still be on the fence, wondering if mushrooms are a viable crop for you to grow. In this chapter, you'll see that they are beyond viable. They are one of the more profitable crops you can have, as they take very little start-up capital. Plus, they fill the downtime on the farm, if you are already growing other vegetables. First of all, we'll look at the benefits of growing mushrooms in general, and then we'll move into a discussion about the profitability of mushroom cultivation.

Benefits of Growing Mushrooms

Since we're going to be looking at profitability next, we won't touch on those benefits in this section. But know that they are just worthy as being in this section as they are the next. There are many benefits to growing mushrooms and very few negatives. The only significant negative is that they can be a difficult crop to raise, and this then can lead you to waste money on something that never takes off. But, with the knowledge in this book, you will be able to minimize this negative to a considerable degree. With that in mind, here are the many pros which far outweigh the cons.

They're Nutritional: If you like eating healthily, then you should absolutely have mushrooms as a part of your diet. They're not called a superfood, but they really should be. Mushrooms are between 5% to 40% protein, depending on whether or not you are eating them fresh or drying them out first. But that's only the beginning. Mushrooms are also packed full of all the essential amino acids that you need in your diet. Plus, vitamin C and vitamin B12. They also have iron, calcium, folic acid, phosphorus, and potassium. This makes them great for you.

But, if you know much about gardening, then you've probably heard of NPK fertilizer. The main nutrients that plants need to grow are nitrogen, phosphorus, and potassium. Mushrooms are high in two of these. This means that mushroom compost can be beneficial for any of the other plants you grow, and for adding nutrients back into the soil. So they're nutritional for you and for your plants.

They're Low Maintenance: Mushrooms can be awkward to grow when you are first getting started; this is true. But once you have a handle on the whole process, it becomes one of the easiest crops. When you're growing vegetables, you typically want to get out into the crop daily to get a sense of how they are doing. You've got to check them for signs of disease and pest infestations. You also need to be careful about not watering them too much.

With mushrooms, you don't need to worry about any of this. Mushrooms are the kind of crop that benefits from being checked less often. In fact, you should only check them once or twice a week. They like to be left in damp and dark areas, so you risk ruining them if you become over-solicitous and start looking at them too often. You still need to be careful when you do check them, but they take far less time and maintenance than your other crops do. That's a terrific time-saver for anyone.

They've Low Cost to Start-up: Growing mushrooms requires you to purchase a few pieces of equipment to begin with, but, for the most part, all of the purchases you make will be one-time costs. That means if it costs you $100 to grow your first batch, it will only cost you $10 to grow your next. Of course, these numbers aren't set in stone but will change depending on what deals you can get and what you already have. The biggest purchase that you'll need to make is a pressure cooker, but that's only if you don't already have one. This is used to obtain a culture from your spores, a sentence that will make more sense after you read Chapter Two and Chapter Five.

Obtaining a culture from spores is a more hands-on and complicated process compared to simply cultivating mushrooms from a spawn, but I recommend that you plan to take the more difficult route. It might have a steeper learning curve, but it is one of those skills which only comes from diving in, as you won't learn to obtain a culture any other way. So, you'll need to purchase a pressure cooker and some spores (or mushrooms you can cut open to obtain spores from). You'll need a substrate to grow the mushrooms in. This is the equivalent of a healthy soil for your vegetables. Other vegetables would hate it, but your mushrooms will think it's terrific. Substrates need to be treated, which may require you to purchase some peroxide or other chemicals, depending on how you want to treat it. You will also need a jar or a container to serve as the growing space itself.

Ultimately, if it weren't for the pressure cooker, it would cost far less to cultivate and grow mushrooms compared to any other vegetable. Even with the pressure cooker, there is far less that needs to be purchased, and this makes it easier to get growing.

MUSHROOM CULTIVATION

They Grow Off Season: If you grow vegetables or crops of your own already, then you know that they are most active during the spring and summer. Once you move into fall, you harvest whatever's left in the ground so that it's all harvested before the first frost of the winter. From that first frost through to the last one in early spring, there's nothing to do but wait around for the chance to start growing again. This downtime might be relaxing, but it means that you're making no money off your agricultural pursuits. If you are growing as a way of earning a living, this equals a slow period where money is often tight.

Mushrooms offer us one way around this. If we want to continue to grow crops in the winter, we don't need to invest in expensive hydroponics systems. Mushrooms cost a lot less to get started with, but they grow throughout the winter so long as you provide them with an ideal environment. But, since they're grown indoors, you have complete control over their environment. What that means is you have a crop that you can sell or consume throughout the winter without having to worry about increasing your electricity bill or going broke in the process.

Can You Profit Growing Gourmet Mushrooms?

The answer to that question is a resounding "YES!"

Gourmet mushrooms are a very, very profitable niche, and they take very little time to cultivate. Admittedly, there is a bit of a learning curve, but once you're over that, you can easily make thousands of dollars growing mushrooms without spending lots of time. There are many growers who do it part-time while they continue to work their full-time jobs. You only need to spend a few minutes checking your crops each week. You can check them daily if you are extremely conscientious, but even checking them seven days a week would only take about fourteen minutes. You'll need to spend a day or two to prepare the crop and a day harvesting down the road, plus another day's worth of work drying and packaging (though this is dependent mainly on the preservation method you choose to employ.) But a couple of afternoons and two or three minutes a day isn't a lot of time. And, as we know, time is money.

Yes, gourmet mushrooms equal money without wasting your time. Right out of the gate, that's amazing. But you're going to need to sell them in order to make that money, so where do you do that?

The biggest purchaser of gourmet mushrooms is always going to be restaurants. One useful tactic is to reach out to local restaurants prior to deciding what to grow and asking them if there are any gourmet mushrooms that they would be interested in purchasing fresh or locally. By doing that, you can work out where the demand is. I have a friend who was a fry cook in a local restaurant. Not a bad job by any means, but it didn't net a lot of money. But he had an idea, and it worked, and now I'd like to convince you of that. He noticed that the restaurant was always looking for interesting and high-quality food. So, he learned how to cultivate gourmet mushrooms and sold them to his work. The first crop netted him more that year than he normally made in four months at his standard job. Within two years, he was selling gourmet mushrooms to six different restaurants, one of which was over an hour and a half drive away, but they were willing to pay for delivery.

One of the reasons that gourmet mushrooms make you so much money is because it only takes a month and a half to grow most varieties to harvest. A short time to mature means you can grow upwards of thirty harvests each year. Plus, if you follow some of the ideas in this book, you can really maximize your space and grow thousands of dollars of mushrooms in a very small area.

If you want to learn just how you can profit from cultivating your own mushrooms, then you're going to want to stick around for Chapter Eight. We'll look at more places you can sell them, as well as some neat ways that you can make your crops go as far as possible. There are a few hints for profiting off gourmet mushrooms that might come as a surprise to you.

MUSHROOM CULTIVATION

Chapter Summary

- Gourmet mushrooms are very nutritional. When dry, they have a very high protein content. They are also jam-packed with essential amino acids, vitamins, and nutrients.

- Mushrooms are high in phosphorus and potassium, which are two of the big nutrients that soil-grown plants require. Mushroom compost can be a great source of nutrients for your garden soil.

- Mushrooms can present a bit of a steep learning curve, but once they are properly spawned, you barely need to check on them.

- Excessive checking on your mushrooms risks their health.

- The largest piece of equipment you need to purchase is a pressure cooker. If you already have access to one, then cultivating mushrooms is especially affordable to begin.

- Mushrooms grow indoors, in a controlled environment. That means you can grow them all year round, summer and winter.

- Gourmet mushrooms are an extremely profitable crop.

- Gourmet mushrooms make a lot of money. They also leave you with plenty of time to work another job or just relax.

- Restaurants will be the prime customer to purchase your mushrooms, but there are plenty of other ways you can earn a profit from these crops.

- Most mushrooms only take about six weeks to grow, so you can have upwards of thirty crops a year and make thousands of dollars.

In the next chapter, we'll take a quick look at the cultivation process. This will be brief and straight to the point in that it will lay out the steps clearly. If you find yourself confused about any of the steps, don't worry. We're going to look at them all carefully as we walk through the entire process.

CHAPTER 2

OVERVIEW OF MUSHROOM CULTIVATION

Cultivating mushrooms is going to take some work. The easiest way for beginners is to purchase a mushroom cultivation kit from one of the many mycological associations or online mushroom businesses. However, we're going to go through the process of obtaining our own cultures rather than purchasing one that is ready to inoculate your substrate.

Step 1: Pick a Species

The first step in the process of mushroom cultivation is the easiest. You are simply going to want to pick a species and begin with it. First-time growers are going to need to get their hands on fresh mushrooms of their chosen variety so that they can either use spores or clone the mushroom itself. Once you have made it through all five steps and harvested your mushrooms, you will have access to plenty of spores and mushrooms for cloning purposes, and so this step becomes even easier.

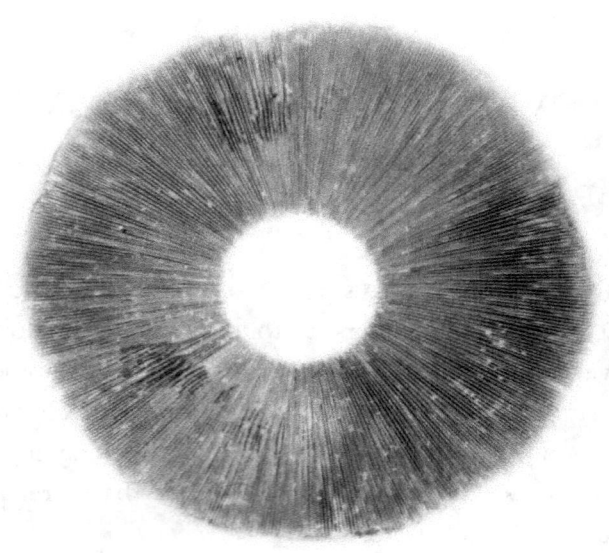

Step 2: Obtain a Culture

Mushrooms will start out either as a clone or a spore. For the most part, we will be looking at spores because they will create a better crop. Spores are taken through the act of a spore print. If the mushroom you are taking a print of has gills, then the spores will be found on the surface of these gills. Mushrooms with pores keep their spores underneath the cap. You take a spore print on the paper so that you can then use it for cultivation.

Spores are placed directly onto a sterile medium and then later transferred to a grain in order to create a spawn. Mixing gelatin and sugar creates a fantastic medium for starting your spore on, but you need to sterilize everything. The pressure cooker is used for this. The gelatin and sugar mixture needs to be boiled to be sterilized. Jars need to be sterilized in the pressure cooker. Tweezers also need to be sterilized in the pressure cooker. You must also use a cleaner on any of the countertops you will be using, and you may want to place tweezers, or any other metal tools you use, into an open flame to ensure they're free of contaminants. Even a little bit of bacteria can ruin the entire process or produce poisonous mushrooms.

Often this step is done with a small petri dish to grow the spores rather than a larger jar. However, a jar with a lid that has been sterilized will offer better protection from bacteria.

Once you're sure everything is scrupulously clean, put the starting medium into sterilized jars. Use your sterilized tweezers to take spores from your spore print (or directly from the mushroom if necessary), and place them on top of this mixture.

You will start to see white tendrils growing on the medium. This is mycelium, and it means that you have a culture on your hands.

MUSHROOM CULTIVATION

Step 3: Prepare Substrate

You will need to decide what you want to grow your mushrooms on. We're going to assume that you go with a typical substance like millet seeds. The culture that we create in the last step will be used to create a spawn, which will be used to grow our mushrooms. But we must have a sterilized growing environment. Using one like millet seed, we need to soak it in water for half a day, and then boil it for sixty minutes to sterilize it. Other substances need to be cleaned in different ways.

It is important to remember that sterilizing the workplace is as important as the grain itself. This is another area in which bacteria can get in and ruin the entire enterprise.

Step 4: Inoculate the Substrate

The mycelium culture you created will need some time to grow and take over. Once it has, it will then be time to use it to inculcate the substrate and create a spawn. This, essentially, is a substance that is inoculated, and so it is described as a spawn; the substance itself doesn't matter in the equation. The mycelium culture is cut into pieces with a sterilized knife and placed into the sterilized jars that have your substrate in them. Seal the jars and shake them well to help mix everything. The spawn jars need to be stored in a dark area at room temperature. They'll need between ten to twenty days so that the mycelium can spread throughout the jar and the substrate.

The substrate will need to be placed in an ideal growing environment. Warm and dark is the most common, but some mushrooms will have more unique needs, so you must research your particular strain beforehand. The mycelium needs to spread throughout the substrate fully. Eventually, you will start to see tiny mushrooms appear. This is called pinning, and these little mushrooms are called primordia. When you see this taking place, you will want to move the mushrooms into a new environment. Rather than promoting the mycelium growth, you now want to promote the fruiting stage of the mushroom's life cycle. You are going to need to be very careful to ensure that the humidity, temperature, light, and even the airflow is all perfectly in line with what the mushrooms need. When you do this, you will grow healthy mushrooms.

There are many different ways in which you can lay out your substrate at this point. You may want to pour it out into a tray, or you may choose to grow in mushroom bags. You can create vertical colonies of mushrooms that grow off small walls. There are many options available, but as long as you are careful about the growing environment, then it is pretty much up to you which is best.

Step 5: Harvest

The final step is to harvest your mushrooms. This is the easiest thing in the world. Harvest them, and then, either use them fresh or dry them out for later. It is up to you.

The more important part of harvesting is that it allows you to take some new spore prints and start the process over again with step one.

MUSHROOM CULTIVATION

Chapter Summary

- The first step to cultivating mushrooms is to choose what species you want.

- You will need to get your hands on some fresh mushrooms of the species you want or get a spore print from another grower.

- As you decide which species to grow, take time to research it and figure out what environmental needs it requires.

- Once you have grown and harvested your mushrooms, you can get plenty of spores to make an even bigger second crop.

- You will need to create a culture. This is done by placing spores on to a sterile mixture.

- A good sterile mixture is gelatin mixed with sugar.

- When working with mushrooms, everything needs to be sterilized. Sterilize the counters you are working on. Sterilize the jars, the tweezers, and any knives you need to use. You can best achieve this by using a pressure cooker.

- Place the sterile mixture into a sterilized jar and let mycelium grow until it takes over the jar.

- Once mycelium takes over the sterilized mixture, you need to transfer it to a substrate jar.

MUSHROOM CULTIVATION

- Substrate needs to be sterilized before it can be used to grow mushrooms. Different substrates will require different steps to sterilize them properly.

- Again, make sure the workspace is clean and sterilized, and not just the tools.

- Next, you need to inculcate the substrate by using a knife to break apart the mycelium and putting it into the substrate jars.

- These jars need to be kept in a dark area at room temperature for between ten to twenty days.

- Once you see mushrooms have begun pinning, move the jars to their ideal growing location so they can fruit and develop fully.

- Substrate can be moved into different locations like trays, bags, or other surfaces so long as they are clean and in the ideal environment.

- Mushrooms should be ready to harvest after roughly six weeks.

- You will be able to get spores and grow lots of new mushrooms after you harvest your own.

In the next chapter, you will learn about the different kinds of mushrooms you can cultivate. These can range from white button mushrooms to matsutake mushrooms, and many more.

CHAPTER 3

CHOOSING YOUR MUSHROOMS

When you order a pizza and select mushrooms, which are usually all the option ever says. Just "mushrooms." This has led to the silly belief that mushrooms are a singular thing. But there are actually lots of different kinds of mushrooms. Maybe you already know what type you want to grow; if so, then you're good to skip ahead to the next chapter to get started setting up a grow room. But if you aren't sure or perhaps just want to learn about some more varieties, then you've come to the right place.

Gourmet mushrooms come in various varieties that range from common and widely loved to more expensive and rare but with a much more niche appeal. To reinforce this split, we will divide this chapter into those more common mushrooms and a couple that are rarer. Right out of the gate, I want to suggest that you stick to those common varieties as a beginner. We'll even take a look at one species that is among the least problematic for beginners to start with. But rare mushrooms are exceedingly difficult to grow, and so we will only look at two examples of these.

Common Varieties

While the following mushrooms are described as common, this doesn't mean that they aren't gourmet or that they don't bring in a delightful little profit. They're common in the way that cheesecake is common. There's plenty around if you go looking, but there are more places that don't have it than those that do. So don't get the wrong idea and think that these mushrooms are less profitable than they are.

Portobello Mushrooms

Portobello mushrooms are huge mushrooms. That's great because they have a lot of nutritional benefits that make them a healthy part of any meal. They're delicious, too, and they go well with steak. Portobellos have become popular in the last few years because they have a lot of protein, and this makes them a healthy alternative to meat for vegetarians and vegans.

Portobello mushrooms can be grown in a fertilizer mix, and they benefit from being spritzed with water. That does make them quite a bit different from the mushrooms we're going to be looking at throughout this book. In fact, you are better off reading about growing vegetables if you are considering portobellos. You can even grow portobellos in an outdoor raised bed garden. They are much, much more resilient to changes in the sun and the temperature, though they will prefer somewhere between 65F and 75F.

Where portobellos differ the most from other raised bed grown vegetables is that it only takes about two weeks after they start pinning for them to be ready for harvest. This is a remarkably quick turnaround, and if you can stagger two crops, then you can pretty much create a stream of revenue with them alone. Portobellos are among the easiest mushrooms to cultivate, and they are a good choice for beginners, but I think there is a better variety to start with.

Oyster Mushrooms

One of the most popular of all the mushrooms there is, oyster mushrooms are a good choice for beginners because they are a little more of a challenge to raise. They will require you to be careful with the sterilization, they will need to be stored in a cool, dark place, and they will require you to move them around to promote better fruiting before harvest. All of these steps make them more complicated than portobellos, but they're not so complicated as to be confusing. By starting with oyster mushrooms, you will be able to get a really solid understanding of mushroom cultivation as a practice rather than just an extension of vegetable farming.

Oyster mushrooms have a savory flavor and have a thin, oyster like appearance from which they take their name. While a common mushroom, they're more expensive than the white button mushrooms that we'll be looking at next. But more expensive means a higher earning per pound, so this is another reason they're a great starting mushroom. They're common enough to be able to get spores easily, but they sell for a tidy little profit.

MUSHROOM CULTIVATION

Oyster mushrooms are a fine addition to many dishes, but especially those that have a lot of sauce. They have a way of soaking up the liquid, and they positively drip with flavor when allowed to do so. They can also be used in stir-fries, or they can be roasted, grilled, fried, baked, or eaten raw. With so many choices, it should be easy to see how many restaurants could benefit from oyster mushrooms. They're a vegetable that can truly fit into most cuisines.

They're low on protein, with only about three grams per cup. But they are also low on carbohydrates and calories, so that's nice. What's even better is the fact that they're bursting with vitamins, and they contain copper, niacin, phosphorus, potassium, and riboflavin. If you are a health nut (or if there are local organic or health food stores nearby to sell to), then you are definitely going to want to start cultivating oyster mushrooms.

You can purchase oyster mushroom kits for an easier time with your first cultivation, but we will be looking at how to prepare all of the pieces necessary to grow oyster mushrooms from spores. But, since you need to get spores first to grow a crop, purchasing an oyster mushroom kit will give you the necessary pieces to grow a small batch, and you can use this batch to raise a much larger one of your own about six weeks later.

White Button Mushrooms

White button mushrooms have a distinct white color, which you'll recognize the second you lay eyes on them. You might not have known what they were called, but you could look at these mushrooms and immediately know that they were okay to eat. The reason for that is because they're included in so many North American dishes that it is actually quite impressive that they still manage to earn a decent amount of money each crop. They are among the lower-earning mushrooms we look at in this book, but they can still earn enough to be worth growing. Of course, I still recommend oyster mushrooms for beginners, but if you call around to local restaurants and find there is a demand for white button mushrooms, then you shouldn't be scared to change your plans and grow these instead.

These mushrooms are quite short but grow to be rather thick. They have a chewy texture and a deep, earthy flavor that makes them a great side dish alongside carrots or turnips. Out of all the common mushrooms we've looked at, these are the most commonly cultivated mushrooms, earning nicknames like "common mushrooms" and "table mushrooms" for their ubiquity. Despite being common, they aren't in any way less nutritious than the others we've looked at. They have antioxidant properties, manganese, zinc, folate, amino acids, phosphorus, riboflavin, and selenium. They can be sauteed, grilled, roasted, baked, eaten raw, or tossed in a stew or a soup. They're often used as part of appetizers or kabobs, though they are also frequently employed on pizza, in stir-fries, or paired with white wine. If you can think up a meal, then it is pretty much a given that white button mushrooms could be added to it and still taste delicious.

White button mushrooms don't like the sunlight, so they're best grown indoors. They can also be grown in manure like portobello mushrooms. That shouldn't come as a surprise, as the two varieties are related to each other. While the spores are developing, they should be kept in a dark and damp location with a temperature of 70F or as close to that as possible. They'll be fine if it's off by five degrees either way. Once the mycelium has taken over the growing space, you should drop the temperature down by fifteen degrees so that it's around 55F. You can expect to be harvesting your button mushrooms about a month after you adjust the temperature. A bed of white button mushrooms should continue to grow in new mushrooms for anywhere from three months to half a year. This is without having to go through the process of spawning more yourself.

MUSHROOM CULTIVATION

Shiitake Mushrooms

More than just a funny name, these mushrooms are extremely delicious, but even more beneficial for health and nutrition than was originally realized. Recent science has revealed shiitake mushrooms to be among the best foods for staying healthy, and this has led to a rise in popularity. They were first cultivated in Asia, but they have been grown in North American for decades. That said, over 80% of all the shiitake mushrooms grown in the world are on the island of Japan. They grow naturally on decaying hardwoods, but we don't need a tree to cultivate them ourselves. What's amazing about them is that you can sell them fresh after harvest, after being dried or being ground up and worked into supplemental forms.

Shiitakes are very small, and so we measure their nutritional value by looking at four of them. They're less than fifty calories, and that's nice, but they only have a gram of protein, which means that there's about a quarter of gram in each mushroom. But there is a ton of copper and vitamin B5, a lot of riboflavin and selenium, and a decent amount of vitamin D, folate, vitamin B6, and magnesium. Plus, they've even got some fiber in them. Oh, and about as many amino acids as you'd find in your hamburger. They have been shown to have anticancer effects, help to lower cholesterol, boost your immune system, and so much more. It's going to get boring real fast if I keep listing the benefits of these remarkable fungi, so I encourage you to take a quick glance at the research being done on these miraculous mushrooms.

As far as how people use them, they are mostly eaten whole. They taste a little bit like meat, but in a slightly bitter way that needs to be complemented by the rest of the meal. That's why they're not often served as a side dish but instead are worked into stir-fries, soups, and other meals that work on a combination of flavors. They're delicious on pizza; you definitely want to try that out sometime. But the other way that shiitake mushrooms are used is supplemental. They're a strong part of herbal medicine practices out of Asia. They've been thought to help keep you healthy for centuries, but science has shown this to be true, and so you can sell ground-up shiitake powders as health supplements, along with the mushrooms themselves.

Shiitake are a very particular mushroom, and so they need a lot of tending to. You'll have to create the perfect environment for them to grow, and this can be quite difficult. As far as beginners go, they would be very challenging. I would suggest working with at least two of the three types we've looked at before you try growing shiitakes. Nonetheless, if you are extremely careful, then you could bring shiitake to harvest, but it is like jumping in at the deep end.

And speaking of the deep end, let's turn our attention over to the expensive mushrooms section of the chapter.

Expensive Mushrooms

These mushrooms sell for a lot, but they are extremely hard to maintain, and, as you'll see, they can have deadly consequences when handled wrong.

MUSHROOM CULTIVATION

Matsutake Mushrooms

This is a rare one. It grows on the west coast of North American for a quarter of the year. But, despite growing in North America, they aren't often eaten here. Instead, they're shipped to Japan because the Japanese love them, and they pay a lot of money for them. They can grow up to six inches tall and eight inches wide, making them a very large and distinct mushroom.

Because they don't grow widely, they aren't common, and

MUSHROOM CULTIVATION

those who live on the East coast of the USA will rarely ever see them in stores. They have a strong, meaty taste, and are primarily fried. The Japanese have worked them into many recipes and created some unique flavors. They are rich in vitamin D, vitamin B3, potassium, and copper. If you can get your hands on one of these mushrooms, you should let them marinate in soy sauce before cooking. Trust me, it will be delicious.

These mushrooms are very awkward to cultivate because they grow on live pine trees. They are considered a wild mushroom, and research is still being conducted to try to cultivate them properly. You may be able to get wild matsutake to start up in your area by spreading spores, but a dedicated crop is still nearly impossible to manage. They're expensive because the demand is hard to match.

Enoki Mushrooms

Enoki are a complicated mushroom. They're tall and thin, and as white as white buttons. They're also used in a lot of Japanese dishes. They're packed full of vitamin B1, vitamin B2, vitamin B3, vitamin B5, iron, copper, calcium, thiamin, phosphorus, selenium, fiber, and amino acids. They've been linked to helping improve your immune system, as well as your digestive tract. They're regarded as useful in slimming. If all that wasn't enough, there's even research that suggests they're excellent for improving your cognitive functions.

They're also responsible for killing four people and getting thirty-two more sick across a dozen states this year. Enoki mushrooms from a specific company were responsible for an outbreak of the disease listeria. This tragic turn of events highlights a vital lesson that you want to keep in mind as you work with mushrooms. These things can be poisonous if they are mishandled. That's why sterilization is such a crucial matter. Of those that we looked at in the common section, the worst that will happen if you mess them up is that they'll go bad. But the rarer the mushroom, the riskier it often is. Do your research before you start growing any new variety and make sure that you understand the risks. Understand the signs that the grow has had problems; that way, you can avoid ever getting or making someone else sick with your mushrooms.

For the time being, please don't try to grow anything dangerous. But as you gain skill, you can start to expand into more specialized varieties like enoki. While it is unfortunate that they have caused people to get sick, it should be noted that those particular mushrooms were imported to the United States. Perhaps the time is near for someone to start growing them on American soil.

Chapter Summary

- There are gourmet mushrooms that are common, and there are those that are rare. While rare sell for more, they are also more of a niche product and harder to move. They are also much harder to grow, and it's recommended that beginners stick with the standard varieties.

- Common gourmet mushrooms still sell for a very respectable price. You can make a ton of money off these varieties because they're always in high demand.

- Portobello mushrooms are a little odd because raising them feels more like growing traditional garden vegetables. In fact, they can even be grown outside in the sun in a raised bed garden next to your lettuce and carrots.

- Portobellos are very high in protein, and this has led to them becoming a popular item in vegetarian and vegan restaurants.

- Portobellos take about two weeks from pinning to harvest.

- Grow portobellos in a temperature range of 65F to 75F.

- Oyster mushrooms get their name from looking like oysters, yet they taste savory.

MUSHROOM CULTIVATION

- Oyster mushrooms sell for a great price, and, while they are a little tricky to grow, they provide a reasonable level of challenge for new growers to get a sense of what mushroom cultivation is all about.

- Oyster mushrooms are used in all sorts of dishes, and they are filled with vitamins and minerals.

- To begin, you can always purchase an oyster mushroom kit. Use this kit to grow your first batch of mushrooms, and then go through the process of sterilization and cultivating a bigger crop from all the fresh spores you've just produced.

- It takes six weeks to bring oyster mushrooms from cultivation to harvest.

- Out of all the mushrooms in this chapter, I recommend starting with oyster mushrooms.

- White button mushrooms are so ubiquitous that they are often referred to as "common mushrooms" or "table mushrooms."

- White button mushrooms are used in a lot of dishes, and this means they're one of the crops that is always in decent demand.

- White button mushrooms should be grown indoors in a damp, dark location.

- White buttons should start out being kept at 70F, but the temperature should be dropped down to

55F once the mycelium has taken over the bed. Four weeks after reducing the temperature, they should be ready for harvest.

- The best part of white buttons is that they continue to produce mushrooms for three to six months, making them a great crop simply for longevity alone.

- Shiitake mushrooms are delicious when served as part of a meal, but they are also highly nutritious.

- Shiitake mushrooms help you to fight cancer, lower your cholesterol, boost your immune system, and they have plenty of vitamins and minerals in them.

- Shiitake mushrooms can be sold fresh, dried, or ground up into a powder to be taken as a health supplement.

- While shiitake are the most impressive of the common gourmet mushrooms, they can be tricky to grow, and it's sensible to try growing the other three varieties before moving on to them.

- Matsutake mushrooms grow in the wild on the west coast of North American, but they are mostly shipped off to Japan.

- They're packed with lots of vitamins and nutrients, a common theme with mushrooms you'll notice.

MUSHROOM CULTIVATION

- If you can get your hands on some, marinate them in soy sauce prior to cooking for a delicious experience.

- Matsutake mushrooms are wild and hard to cultivate, even when attempted by experts.

- Enoki mushrooms are native to Japan.

- Enoki are packed with four different kinds of B vitamins and have been shown to improve your immune system. They help with digestion and even the functioning of the brain.

- Unfortunately, Enoki was responsible for an outbreak of listeria in the United States this year. You should not try to grow any mushroom that can be harmful when mishandled

- There are many mushrooms that can turn poisonous when they are grown improperly. Stick to the common variations of mushrooms we've mentioned; these simply go bad rather than turn deadly.

- Any time you start growing a new type of mushroom that you haven't encountered before, you should do your research. Of course, you want to do this to see how best to raise them, but you should also keep an eye out for possible side-effects. Always, always take the time to research and understand the risks.

In the next chapter, you will learn how to set up a growing

space for your mushrooms. From ensuring the environment is safe to taking care of the humidity, temperature, lighting, and airflow, everything you need to consider when designing your grow room is covered.

CHAPTER 4

SETTING UP A GROW ROOM

In this chapter, we're going to set up our grow rooms. The plural is very appropriate here as there are actually multiple spaces used in cultivating mushrooms. Sometimes you may use one space for the entire process, but this is only really tenable when growing on a very small scale, such as when using a single, sealable container. More often than not, these spaces are going to be separated from each other. This may mean that you close off the corner of the overall grow room for the purpose of serving as a lab, but you could also dedicate a specific room to be your lab if you wanted. Or, depending on your approach, you might even remove the lab entirely.

We'll look at three pieces of your mushroom cultivation space. These are the lab, the preparation area, and the grow room itself. We'll see why we use each one, and what we need to set them up to make our mushroom growing as smooth an experience as possible. In the next chapter, we will be looking at different growing methods. Some of these will bypass the need for a laboratory or even a truly dedicated grow room. So, before you start building your grow room, make sure you read Chapter Five as well. That way, you know exactly how much space you need for your particular approach before you find yourself spending unnecessary time and funds.

The Laboratory

The first step in the mushroom growing process is the hardest. At this stage, when you are trying to go from simple spores to a mushroom mycelium, it is important beyond belief that you keep everything as clean as can be. That's already been mentioned, but it can't be emphasized enough. Different growing mediums can be used here, but, most of the time, operations are done with petri-dishes filled with a little bit of grain, agar, or even a sugar mixture, as we've briefly discussed previously. These mixtures are rich in nutrients, and they are also quite moist. That is necessary to make them a suitable home for mushroom mycelium to grow, but it is also, unfortunately, a perfect host for bacteria and molds. As soon as a mold takes hold, you can kiss the mushroom mycelium goodbye.

The laboratory in a mushroom operation is a space that is dedicated purely to this early stage of mushroom cultivation. It is therefore treated almost as an off-limits area. Reducing the foot traffic in the laboratory is necessary to keep it clean, so the area should reflect this. Blocking off a corner of your kitchen isn't a very good idea for a laboratory, but setting aside that extra broom closet at the end of the hallway would work. However, for the best results, you should pick an area with walls that are easy to clean. Everything you bring into the room is going to be wiped down and cleaned often, but, if at all possible, you want walls and floors that can be cleaned with a little bit of watered down bleach. Cleanliness is the rule of any laboratory.

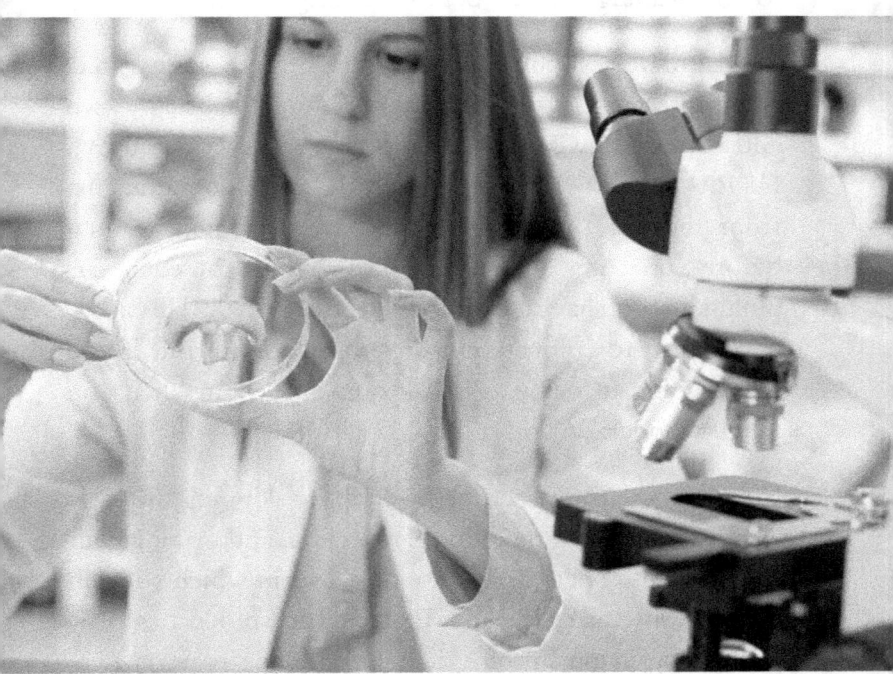

Cleanliness also begins with you, not the laboratory. One of the reasons that the laboratory should be closed off from the surrounding environment is so that you remember to always clean yourself before entering. Wear clean clothes, wash your hands, or wear sterile gloves. You may even consider using a zippered partition to create an "airlock" between the lab and the rest of the building. If you keep everything sterile inside the laboratory and are always cleaning before and after working in it, then the only risk you will run is introducing harmful bacteria due to not cleaning yourself before entering.

The laboratory should have a surface space. Stainless steel is ideal because it is easy to clean. Enough lighting to see and a strong flow hood are important. A flow hood uses a HEPA filter in order to remove harmful contaminants from the air. By keeping the space separate, cleaning before you enter, and using a flow hood to reduce air pollutants, you have a wonderfully effective lab. This is key if you plan to cultivate mushroom mycelium. But if you aren't going to cultivate mushroom mycelium, then you might wonder: do you still need a lab?

You can get around setting up a lab by skipping the early steps of cultivating mushroom mycelium and making your own spawns. There are plenty of places in which you can purchase premade spawns. In fact, you should begin by purchasing a mushroom kit or a premade grain spawn. What that does is allow you to get started far quicker and go through the steps of growing and harvesting your own mushrooms. This first purchase will give you a harvest from which you can produce plenty of spores to cultivate the next batch. However, you can't cultivate that next batch without having a laboratory. So, while it may be the case that you might not use it immediately, you will find that you'll want to have a laboratory by the time that harvesting comes around.

I believe that a laboratory is necessary for a well-functioning mushroom operation. The work you do in the laboratory will give you hands-on experience for each and every step in the growth of your mushrooms. You will be able to produce much larger harvests by increasing the size of your spawns when you have a laboratory, whereas ordering premade spawns will limit your size. You can always purchase more spawns for a bigger harvest, but this quickly costs more money than it is worth. A laboratory will rapidly pay for itself when you compare the difference in profit ratio between cultivating your own spawns versus buying premades.

MUSHROOM CULTIVATION

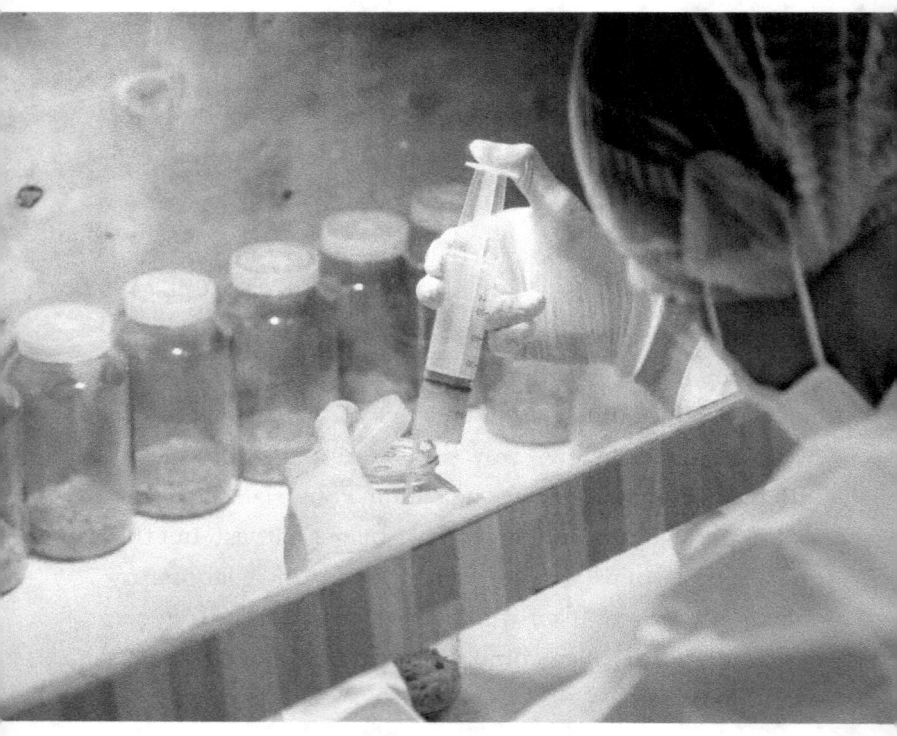

If you cannot dedicate an entire space to serve as a lab, then you can get away with using another location so long as you are extremely fastidious about cleaning it beforehand. A flow hood can be placed on most surfaces, and so you can turn the dining room table into a temporary lab if you need to. The downside is that when you work in a space like this, it is much easier to get infected cultures. It is important to research what healthy mycelium of the species you are working with looks like. When you know what it is supposed to look like, it is much easier to tell when something has gone wrong. Makeshift labs will see a much greater rate of failure, but you yourself are still the most likely to cause the infection. Clean yourself before working in your lab, especially when that lab is makeshift.

The Preparation Area

The next area you will need is the preparation area. This can be as simple as your kitchen or as complicated as you can possibly imagine. For our purposes, we're going to stay on the simple side. This area needs to be kept clean, but not nearly to the extent that the lab does. What equipment you need inside your preparation area is going to be determined by the species of mushroom you are growing and what material makes for the best spawns for that particular species. The most common spawns are grain spawns, but you could also be using sawdust or straw.

If you are using grain, then you will want to have a sink or a tub available as part of the preparation is to soak the grain. The larger your growing operation is, the more space you are going to want for soaking. Grain also needs to be heated up as well, so you will want a source of heat in the area. Small scale operations can use the kitchen sink and the stove, which makes it a little easier to get started cultivating. Regardless of whether you are doing grain or not, every preparation area should have a way of sterilizing the jars or bags being used for growing. You can use a stovetop pressure cooker as we previously discussed, but another option is to get a larger pressure sterilizer. This piece of equipment is much larger than the stovetop one, so much so that you will need to dedicate a space just to it. But, if you are growing on a large scale, then it is an investment that you'll probably want to make sooner rather than later.

The best space for a preparation area, in my opinion, is just out in the backyard. You don't need to be worried about keeping out bacteria as you do in the lab, so as long as you keep the space clean, then it works well. It's best to have a tarp or even some patio covering for protection against the elements. You can certainly use a garage or a shed as a preparation area, but you need to be careful when you start to use a pressure sterilizer. They release lots of hot steam,

steam that has been pressurized, and this can easily cause bodily harm as well as property damage if you aren't careful. Setting up outside can help to limit the possibility of fire, a nightmare of an experience for anyone, let alone those who have a farm inside their home.

As mentioned before, you may have your lab in the same space as another area, such as the preparation area. For example, consider designating your garage as your space for growing mushrooms. You have a large room, but you only need a small space for your lab. Therefore, you partition a small section off from the rest of the room, and there you have your lab. The rest of the space can then be used as a preparation area. However, if you decide to set your preparation area outside, then you can in no way use the same space as part of the lab. The more extensive your growing operation, the more space you are going to need for your preparation area. In contrast, a lab only needs to grow in size at about a quarter of the rate as your preparation space does. So, when you are designating a space for your preparation area, consider if it offers the possibility of expansion. It may be better to set up a separate lab rather than limit the space you have for prep.

Striking the right balance size for your preparation area is one of the elements which growers need to discover for themselves. Most begin by using their kitchen, but they quickly grow too large for this to be effective. If you are starting out with your operation, sticking with your kitchen is a smart idea. But you should be aware of how quickly the need for space grows when you start earning a profit from your mushrooms.

Grow Room

The grow room you choose is going to be determined by the species of mushrooms you grow, combined with the method of cultivation that you decide on. Before the end of the chapter, we will take a look at two easy grow room setups. But, before we worry about that, we should understand the goal of the grow room itself. Obviously, it needs to be a physical space for us to keep our mushrooms. If we are growing mushrooms in bags, then we need a way to either shelf them or to hang them up. This could mean adding shelving or simply stringing up secure wiring from which you can tie and hang plastic grow bags.

MUSHROOM CULTIVATION

How much space you need in your grow room depends on not only the size of your operation but also the species. There are some types of mushrooms that grow best on logs. Some growers create rafts out of these logs and then spread out their mushrooms over the top of them. That will require a lot of floor space, as many of these logs are five feet or more in length. Species that can be grown in bags offer a great way of maximizing the space. Grow bags tend to be pretty big, but you can typically hang two above each other in the same place. If you are careful in picking the particular mushrooms you are growing, you may find it is most useful to have a variety of growing methods employed at the same time. On one side of the grow room, you may have bags while you have shelves and logs on the other. Fitting together lots of mushrooms is easy physically, but it is much harder to pull off environmentally.

Speaking of the environment, your grow room is going to need a tightly controlled environment. Cultivating mushrooms requires us to have total control over the CO_2, temperature, and humidity of the grow room. Controlling the temperature is the easiest to do indoors, though you may need to use a cooling system or a space heater depending on whether or not you have a heating system that lets you fine-tune individual rooms. If you are growing outside in a shed or a barn, then these pieces of equipment become a necessity.

Mushrooms most often want a cool temperature, though there are some that enjoy warm weather. But most of the mushrooms you will be growing will want the temperature to be on the cool side, around the 60F range. Some species need to be tricked into thinking that it is time for them to start fruiting. We achieve this by dropping their temperature so that they think the time of year has changed. When growing multiple species of mushroom, you need to be aware of whether or not you will need to cold shock any of them. Two different species may enjoy a similar growing environment, but if one needs to be cold shocked and the other doesn't, then you run the risk of killing one of the species to ensure the other fruits. Always research all of the temperature needs of your species before you begin.

CO2 is controlled by introducing fresh air into the grow room. Fresh air is an important part in the growth of your mushrooms, just the same way as oxygen is one of the major nutrients required by most vegetables. How much fresh air a mushroom needs is determined by the species, but there are some physiological effects that occur depending on the amount of fresh air present. If your mushrooms don't get enough fresh air, then you can expect them to produce small caps but tall stems. There are species in which this is the desired outcome, but the vast majority of gourmet mushrooms that you'll be growing want to have nice, large caps. Fresh air is introduced into the growing space by using a fan that is connected to air outside the room. It doesn't help us to add a fan that simply recirculates the stale air of the room. If it isn't pulling in air from outside, then it is of no help to us.

Humidity is also an important factor in creating the ideal environment for your mushrooms. When growing vegetables, there is often a point in which you may need a dehumidifier to help you out. With mushrooms, you are pretty much always going to need to pump more humidity into the grow space rather than remove it. One of the big reasons for this is that all the fresh air serves to reduce the humidity level. Your mushrooms need that humidity, though. If there isn't enough humidity in the grow room, then the mushrooms may not develop, or if they do, then they'll be disfigured. Too much humidity will promote problems with bacteria. To remove humidity from the grow space, simply turn off the humidifier and let the fresh air bring down the levels. The species will determine the level of humidity, but, generally, most mushrooms want to be right around 90%.

Along with controlling the environment of the grow room, you also need it to be as clean as possible. While it doesn't need to be as clean as the laboratory, you should try to keep it close to this standard. Always clean yourself before going into the grow room, and never track in dirt or gunk on your clothes. If you are working outside in your clothing, change to something clean prior to entering the grow room. Use equipment that you can wipe down and clean with sterilizing chemical cleaners. You will want to be able to clean the walls, countertops, and even the floor. When you are first building your grow room, you should always be asking yourself if you can thoroughly clean any equipment before you bring it in.

Of course, this discussion has looked at grow rooms as entire rooms. This is necessary for a growing operation of any real size, but there are two easy ways to get started that we'll look at now. Keep in mind that you can easily expand on the following approaches and use them to make up just a small part of your grow room.

Creating a Quick Growing Environment

When you are beginning with your mushroom farm, it is

highly unlikely that you are going to set aside a large grow space. Your first grow will probably be quite small, and you are even unlikely to need a lab as you'll probably be happy to stick with a grow kit. At this stage, your best bet isn't to invest a lot of time or money into your operation. Instead, you should purchase only what you need to get the job done. That will allow you to see a good portion of the growing cycle of mushrooms and really get a sense of the work that goes into it. If you find that you enjoy the work or that it is highly profitable, then you are more likely to invest your resources into creating a proper growing operation.

We're going to look at two growing setups that you can use to get started. In fact, you can create the first one and then upgrade it to the second down the road. The other setup we look at will be very valuable in the long run, and you may want to consider using a series of them in a larger grow room. But before we get into that, let's start with the simplest way to create a growing environment.

Single Container Growing Environment

By far the easiest way to get started with mushroom cultivation is to use a single container. Any clear plastic container works, but you are best off going with one the size of a laundry basket. It will still ultimately prove to be far too little space for any kind of long-term growing operation, but it is large enough for a sizable harvest your first time out. Not counting the equipment necessary for sterilizing the workspace or growing media, a single container growing environment can easily cost less than $20 depending on where you shop. You will want a see-through plastic container, something to make holes in it, some perlite to create a base, and a spray bottle that emits a really fine mist.

The first step is to drill or cut holes into the container. Drill holes along the four walls of the container, spacing them to be about two inches apart. This grid of holes is how fresh air gets into the mushrooms. It is best to use a fan that brings in air from the outside, but you can save money by placing your growing environment near a window. Sun can be beneficial for some species, but you shouldn't let your mushrooms have full access. It is better to keep the curtains closed so that the light is diffused. You'll need to keep careful track of the temperature, and the humidity levels are also equally important. You can track both of these by using a hygrometer, killing two birds with one stone.

Maintaining the humidity in a single container is much cheaper than it is to maintain a whole grow room. We start by making a base of perlite at the bottom of the container. It should take up between one fifth and one-quarter of the overall growing environment. Before putting it in, make sure to soak the perlite in water first. This rock absorbs and holds on tightly to water, and this raises the humidity of the growing space. You will need the spray bottle to keep the humidity level night and high. Opening up the container and misting it is the only way to control the humidity. Since you're the one in charge of the misting, you are going to need to check on your mushrooms several times a day. Often you can need to mist two, three, or even four times a day.

Cultivating your mushrooms is very straightforward in this system. You will simply put your spawn into the container and then look after it. Building this single container growing environment only takes ten or twenty minutes, depending on what you use to make the holes. It'll take an hour of soaking in water before the perlite is ready to put in, but you can put it in the sink and go and do other things while it soaks. The biggest downside to this method is that it requires extra time and attention to ensure that everything fruits properly. It is also not a viable option for those looking to grow big crops, as it simply does not have the space necessary. But a single container growing environment is the cheapest, easiest way to start cultivating mushrooms, and it requires only a minimal amount of building to get going. That makes it great for beginners to get a sense of what raising mushrooms is all about.

MUSHROOM CULTIVATION

Mini-Greenhouse: A Multi-Tiered Growing Environment

This option is the midway point between a single container growing environment and a grow room. This approach is more expensive than the single container approach, but it gives plenty of space for a lot more mushrooms per crop. More mushrooms equal more profit. You can get a fine enough multi-tiered greenhouse for anywhere from $20 to $40. If you are particularly handy, then you may even consider making your own using PVC piping. There are many video guides online which you can find for step by step instructions. However, at such a low cost, it can be worth spending the extra $10 or $20 to save the time it takes for preparation. Regardless of how you make it, the result is going to be the same.

These mini-greenhouses have become popular with gardeners as they are a cheap way of creating an ideal environment for starting seeds indoors. Rather than dedicate a room to creating a growing environment, these mini-greenhouses create a self-contained environment so you can sit them in your kitchen, living room, bedroom, or closet and not have to worry about the environment of the room itself. A proper mini-greenhouse will come with a zippered covering. Sometimes this covering is an opaque material, but for mushrooms, it is best to use a see-through plastic. This covers the entire greenhouse from top to bottom so that temperature and humidity can be trapped inside. You will need to be mindful of the temperature of the space in your mini-greenhouse, but the humidity levels will be a lot easier to maintain.

While you'll want to purchase a hygrometer for your mini-greenhouse, you won't need to rely on perlite and a spray bottle to keep the humidity levels in check. Instead, buy a small ultrasonic humidifier. This type of humidifier raises the humidity level by creating hot vapors. The other type of humidifier, a cool-mist humidifier, will work a lot slower and is ultimately nowhere near as effective. While you want the humidity level to range anywhere between 75% and 95%, you don't want it to be at 100%. That means you can't just merely switch on the humidifier and leave it alone. If you want to avoid having to check on the humidity often, you should get a humidifier that has a timer setting or get a timer for the outlet itself. You will still need to pay close attention to the levels when you are starting, but, given a little bit of time and experimentation, you will eventually be able to leave the humidifier alone once you have the perfect timing down.

Because of the humidity level, it is not a good idea to let your mini-greenhouse stand freely. Moisture from the humidifier will damage hardwood. Worse still, carpeted floors can mold and promote the growth of harmful bacteria. You should lay down a plastic tarp at the very least, but the best option is to use a small plastic tub. What a tub does is catch excess moisture and keeps it from possibly spilling the way a tarp might. That's doubly true for those times when you need to add a fan to the setup. Not every species of mushroom will need a fan, but those that require lots of oxygen will want the extra fresh air, and this can easily cause spills if the floor isn't protected by a raised surface such as the walls of a tub.

Less oxygen hungry species will be able to get by with the fan attached to the humidifier, but you may want to consider directing this flow more precisely through the use of PVC piping. If you place the humidifier inside of the greenhouse, then you end up recirculating the same air. By using PVC piping, the air the humidifier pumps out is from outside of the growing environment, and thus it removes CO_2 and introduces oxygen. The best part of using PVC piping is that it allows us to set up a second greenhouse easily. We need to purchase or make the second greenhouse itself, but we can use a T-jointed piece of PVC pipe to let our humidifier service two greenhouses. This allows us to very easily double the amount we are growing without having to increase our costs significantly. Keep in mind that adding a second greenhouse is going to change the timings for your humidifier, and it is unlikely that it will create enough airflow to support both, so a fan will be necessary. It is also easy to stick two of these greenhouses together, though you will need to purchase or make a new plastic covering to contain the growing environment.

So, while there is room to scale up your mini-greenhouse very simply, it is worth considering how much a single greenhouse can grow. That is going to depend on how many shelves you have. The most common designs to be found are the three or four shelf versions. Each shelf gives you the equivalent of a single container growing environment. Therefore, you can produce three or four times as much with a dedicated mini-greenhouse. The reason for this is the way that it uses vertical space. In the single container environment, the mushrooms are only going to grow on the top of everything. That creates a space between the top of the mushrooms and the lid, and the bottom fifth or fourth of the container is filled simply with perlite. The perlite is only used to keep the humidity, so we don't need to use any perlite at all. This means that we can just take out a baking sheet and spread out grain spawn on it. We can slot one or two of these sheets per shelf, depending on what size we have available.

As this approach costs more, it isn't recommended for those who are unsure whether mushroom farming is for them or not. But, if you are already sure that you want to get into this field, then I recommend beginning with one of these mushroom greenhouses. They're easy to expand, and the parts are useful pieces of a grow room. You can move the greenhouse into a future grow room as your operation expands. The single container growing environment can also be moved into a grow room, but it quickly becomes pointless to keep wasting time to set up a single container when you can do four times as much with less than half the effort.

Chapter Summary

- There are three different rooms which make up a full mushroom growing operation. You can get away without any of them if you are growing only small batches and are extremely careful. But anybody producing for profit is going to want to be able to dedicate some space specifically for mushroom cultivation.

- The three rooms are the laboratory, the preparation area, and the grow room itself.

- The laboratory is used to grow spores into spawns. This process requires that the space and all the equipment used are sterilized and cleaned. Laboratories should be given their own space so that they can be kept secure and safe. It is always easier to keep a laboratory clean than it is to try to save your crops when they're infected this early.

- Sterilize the lab before working with spores, and then again afterward as part of your offboarding process. Always wash your hands before coming in. Walls you can clean with bleach are a plus, and the same with the floors. Surface space should be stainless steel.

- Get a flow hood for working with the spores and early fungal growth. This helps to keep airborne pollutants from infecting your samples.

- If you aren't making your own spawns, then you can get by without needing a lab. You can do lab work on a table in your house so long as you can sterilize it and use a flow hood for safety.

- A preparation area is necessary for large operations. A tub or sink is perfectly fine for soaking grain when you are beginning, but the more you grow, the larger the space that is going to be necessary. You may also want to get a good-sized pressure sterilizer. They give off lots of hot air so they should be kept outdoors, or at least in areas that are not flame risks when heated.

- Because of the flame risk, I like to use the backyard as a preparation area. I can rest easy knowing the pressure sterilizer isn't going to cause any damage. Patio coverings can be used to keep everything safe from wind and rain.

- Your grow room is the area in which the mushrooms themselves will grow. The lab is also used to grow, so it could technically be called a grow room, but it is several steps removed from the mushrooms themselves.

- Grow rooms can be created as full rooms or small portable "rooms" that you can set up throughout the house. How much space you need for your operation depends on how large it is. Having an area in which you can control the temperature, humidity, and CO_2 levels will give you the best control. If you control the temperature and humidity of a room, then you can control the CO_2 levels by introducing fresh air from outside the room.

MUSHROOM CULTIVATION

- You can create full rooms, but when starting your operation, it is best to begin small and scale your way up. Beginning with a single container growing environment, you can move onto a mini-greenhouse, and then you can put multiple mini-greenhouses together to create a full grow room.

- A single container growing environment is a plastic container that has had holes drilled into it every two inches in a grid-like pattern. Soaked perlite is poured into the bottom of the container, and the growing substrate and mushroom mycelium is put on top. Use a spray bottle to maintain the humidity level. You'll find this a cheap and easy way to grow mushrooms.

- A mini-greenhouse is a multi-level plant rack that uses a zipped plastic covering to keep the humidity trapped in. They can be made from PVC pipe or bought online for around $40. Fresh air is piped in by a fan kept nearby. The humidity level is left high through the use of an ultrasonic humidifier.

In the next chapter, you will learn about the different growing methods available to use when cultivating your mushrooms. We'll explore the approaches for developing specific species, and then move on to discussing how each general method of growing is achieved.

CHAPTER 5

GROWING METHODS

As with most agriculture, there are a variety of methods that can be used. Some of these methods are specific to particular mushroom species; others are concerned more with the space you have available to you. This chapter will explore the idea of growing methods from several angles. The first is the cultivation process as it relates to different species. We'll look at shiitake, oyster, button, and paddy straw mushrooms here. From there, we'll look at outdoor beds and rafts, indoor systems, and even growing mushrooms in a bag. We will go through the entire process of raising our mushrooms in the following chapter.

Cultivation Methods by Species

An idea that I would like my readers to take on board is the simple fact that every species of mushroom is different. One may have similarities to another, but none of them are precisely the same. It is important never to assume we have knowledge about a species merely because we've worked on similar ones. Consider if other professionals applied this same logic. Your heart doctor isn't the person you want looking at your brain, and you don't ask Jimmy from IT to repair your dialysis machine. Assumptions in these areas may kill you just the same way that assumptions about your mushrooms will leave them dead. We're going to look at four different species to see how they grow best and how they differ from one another. The different approaches applied to these species will point us towards the second half of the chapter, where we will be looking more closely at growing methods themselves rather than particular strains.

Oyster Mushrooms: Oyster mushrooms are among the easiest to start with. In Nature, they grow on collapsed trees, which make them ideal for a raft method approach. Oyster mushrooms are often raised by sawing off a part of a log, inoculating the cut, and then nailing the whole thing back together. In a raft approach, it makes more sense to inoculate the locations where the logs come together. The logs used for oyster mushrooms should be moist, if not completely soaked. The inoculated logs are wrapped in black plastic garbage bags along with wet sand, and these packages are left in a cool area. In about a month or so, your oyster mushrooms will begin to fruit.

MUSHROOM CULTIVATION

When you use the raft approach or open-air methods of growing on logs, you need to be able to keep everything together and maintain the right temperature and humidity. That requires a grow room rather than just a small space. If you are growing oyster mushrooms, but don't have a grow room, then you should use the bag approach. You can skip logs entirely if you want to grow in bags or beds. Sawdust or straw are popular substrates for oyster mushrooms. The substrate you choose should be mixed with limestone so that the overall weight of the mixture is

1% limestone. This is done to change the pH level. Pasteurize the entire mixture before inoculation. You want anywhere from 2% to 5% of the final weight of the mixture to come from the inoculum. That will give you a final weight made up of a ratio of 94% substrate, 5% inoculum, and 1% limestone. This mixture will take about the same amount of time, but it can be put into bags, containers, bottles, beds, trays, tubs, or whatever else you have for holding your growing mushrooms.

Shiitake Mushrooms: Shiitake mushrooms are tasty and nutritious mushrooms that also like to grow on logs. They want hardwood logs, and healthy ones at that, which makes them a little more picky than oyster mushrooms are. This is made especially clear when you see just how particular they are. You need to start with a hardwood log that is roughly 4 inches in diameter and about four feet long. This log should be soaked prior to the next step. When the log is properly soaked, it is time to drill holes. It's best to do that with an electric drill as you'll want many holes. Inoculum made out of sawdust is put into the holes, about an inch deep into the log. Use wax to seal off the holes. This wax is also used on the ends of the log during the drier months so that the log can more easily retain moisture. Logs are usually stacked diagonally, or they are set up in a triangle fashion. Once stacked, they are covered with plastic to keep the humidity levels high.

The best part of growing shiitake mushrooms like this is the minimal amount of maintenance required. It'll take about two months for them to be ready to fruit, but during that time, you only need to do a check a month. This growing environment is ideal for a green fungus called trichoderma. Check once a month to make sure there is none. After about two months, you'll start to see mycelium spreading out from the cracks around the holes and from the ends of the logs. You don't want to introduce any extra moisture into the equation during this period. Some mushrooms need a cold shock to encourage them to start fruiting, but shiitakes need a bath. Once the mycelium has spread far and wide, you take the logs down and soak them. That will trigger the shiitake's fruiting impulse, and, as the logs dry, you'll begin to see your mushrooms pin.

Shiitake logs can be a bit annoying when you are getting started. They don't always fruit the first year around. But the cool thing about this approach is that the logs can continue producing shiitake crops for half a decade or more.

Button Mushrooms: Button mushrooms are a staple of many a meal, and one of the reasons for this is how closely they align with other farming practices. Button mushrooms grow on composts and manure. This makes them an easy addition to just about any farm, be it vegetable or livestock. Pasteurize the compost you will be using and then spread your spawn out over it. You want to have a pound of spawn per square yard. That means a ratio of 1:160. It is very easy to tell when your button mushroom mycelium is ready to induce fruiting. The top of your mushroom bed should be at least half mycelium so that more surface is mycelium than compost. To induce fruiting, the bed is covered with a peat and lime mixture that has a pH level of 7.0. You can add another layer of spawn on top of this, but the results can be mixed. Sometimes it helps create a bigger yield, but oftentimes it proves to be a waste of good spawn. Keep this at around a temperature of 75F.

Ten or so days after you have covered the bed, you will start to see your mushroom pin. When you see pinning, reduce the temperature to 60F. That assists your mushrooms to fruit more fully. It takes button mushrooms about ten days to go from pinning to harvest. These mushrooms lend themselves well to outdoor beds, though you need to be mindful of the weather to get the full effects of a dropping temperature.

MUSHROOM CULTIVATION

Paddy Straw Mushrooms: These appetizing Chinese mushrooms are grown primarily on banana leaves and rice straw. The banana leaves can be tricky to get depending on where you live, but rice straw is quite affordable. Take some newspaper and soak it in 2% urea. Use this to wrap around 18-inch packages of the straw. These are stacked one per shelf. These can be done outdoors, and if you live in a rainy area, then you won't need to water them. Dry weather will require watering. You start to water about a week after you have set the packages, and you continue to water each day until the mushrooms begin to pin. About two weeks later, they should be ready for harvest.

Paddy straw mushrooms are a fine choice if you are planting outdoors. You can easily create a full raised bed of paddy straw mushrooms and get 20+ pounds a harvest from them. They fit in well with a chicken farm since a compost of chicken manure and rice straw creates an excellent growing environment, so long as everything is pasteurized. Despite this, it is most common to simply use the above method to produce a bountiful harvest.

Growing Methods

In the previous section, we used terms like "raft" when describing ideal growing conditions for oyster mushrooms. In this section, we'll look at rafts, as well as a few other methods for growing your mushrooms. Where the last section looked at species and discussed the methods best for them, this one will look at the methods first, and then discuss which species work best for it.

Outdoor Mushroom Beds: Outdoor beds are a good choice for mushrooms like portobellos, wine caps, inky caps, blewits, and more. To start with, any mushroom that grows well on fertilizer can fit an outdoor bed. You could dedicate ground in your yard for these beds, but I will always recommend the use of raised garden beds, as they give you a much higher level of protection and control over the growing environment. You'll need to put together the beds using untreated lumber or full logs, and this eats up a fair bit of time in the beginning. But, once you've constructed a raised bed, you can use it for decades with only a minimal need for repairs.

Before you settle into making your raised beds, there are a handful of considerations you must not ignore. Raised beds can be moved if necessary when they are made out of a lighter material, but the heavier the material, the harder they are to relocate. That means you need to be cautious when picking a location, as the amount of sunlight, shade, and wind protection are all significant factors, and different mushrooms will have different needs. Make sure that you research the mushrooms you are going to grow in these beds long before you make the beds or buy the substrate. Keep in mind that a raised garden bed should be no larger than four feet wide; otherwise, harvesting is going to be particularly awkward. These considerations will slow down your initial experience, but it is always better to prepare thoroughly before you jump into any type of growing.

The best thing about outdoor beds is that they can produce mushrooms for years, and it is very easy to double up your use of space. That first point is going to be determined by what species you grow, but some will continue to grow for nearly a decade after the initiation inoculation. The second point, the maximization of space, requires a little bit more effort on our parts, but it makes outdoor beds an amazing opportunity for growers. Most of the time that we make raised garden beds, we pick our material for its sturdiness, cost, or aesthetics. If we are willing to wait a little bit longer before starting our beds, then we can make the beds themselves a viable growing environment for mushrooms. Take and fully inoculate some hardwood logs with reishi or shiitake. Once the logs are fully inoculated, use them to build the raised bed. Reishi will need to be in contact with soil to fruit, so fill up the beds with soil. From there, you can use the top of the bed with compost or wood chips; in fact, whatever growing medium is necessary. This gives you a raised garden bed that produces mushrooms both on the outside and the inside. This simple trick can quickly multiply your earnings; just make sure that you use logs that are correctly inoculated so as to avoid fungal contamination.

MUSHROOM CULTIVATION

Rafts: A raft is a good fit for mushrooms like brick tops, maitake, nameko, reishi, and pioppinos. While these use inoculated logs as the main growing medium, they still require a bit of help from other materials. This means that rafts aren't exactly as simple as just "growing some mushrooms on a log," but they aren't overly complicated, thankfully. The biggest thing with using the raft method is that you need to be careful with the space you choose, and you must have patience getting started. However, you can use this method indoors or outdoors. We'll be focusing on the outdoor approach here.

Rafts take to the outdoors even better than raised garden beds. When we are growing with a raised garden bed, we are still aiming at getting some decent sun. If we decided that we didn't want to keep growing mushrooms, then it is straightforward for us to empty a raised garden bed so that it can be used to grow other fruits and vegetables. That makes it highly unlikely that we'd ever normally build a raised garden bed in that dank, sun-starved corner of the back yard. Of course, your own "no man's land" might not be in the back corner, but just about every homeowner has that one section of their yard where pretty much nothing wants to grow. That section, a major pain in the past, is actually perfect for some mushroom rafts.

It can take a few months for logs to be completely inoculated. When making rafts, you want to be sure that your logs are fully inoculated before you take them outdoors. We take this precaution for the same reason we only use fully inoculated logs for our raised garden beds. If we only use partially inoculated logs, then we are providing a space for other molds to grow. Molds will almost universally outpace the growth of mushrooms, and thus destroy the crop by using up the same resources. Depending on the species you are growing, you will have a wait of weeks or months before your logs are ready to use. Rather than waste this time, it presents a good opportunity to investigate that back corner you're going to be growing your mushrooms in.

It should be easy to watch the sunlight and see exactly how much gets through to this area. It's best if it is shaded throughout the day, though you can always add some covering for extra shade if needed. It is always easier to remove light than it is to add it in. This serves us well since we won't need any for this growing method. More frustrating is the soil itself. We may or may not use the natural soil when it comes time to build the raft proper, so we need to take the time to ensure it is healthy. Get yourself a soil test kit and run samples of the soil from the selected area. If the soil is healthy, then you have nothing to worry about. If it is filled with heavy metals, then the soil is considered contaminated, and it isn't suitable for growing mushrooms as they like to soak these heavy metals up. Heavy metals aren't good when growing traditional vegetables, as they can cause harm to those that ingest them, but they are even worse when it comes to mushrooms because they love absorbing them all. If the soil is contaminated, then you'll have to purchase a plastic tarp, preferably a thick one, and cover it with healthy soil. This will be the bedding for our rafts.

You will be able to tell the logs are ready once the mycelium has begun to sprout out of the ends. Mycelium growth will first be visible around the holes or areas that you originally inoculated. This growth is important because it shows us that it is working, but we must wait until it reaches both ends of the logs before we get too excited. When it has, simply take out the logs, and create a small raft by laying them side by side on the tarp you've prepared. If your soil was healthy already, then you won't need the tarp and can place them right on the soil. Next, depending on the species of mushroom, you'll want to pour wood chips, straw, or another medium onto them to help promote growth. Some species, such as the reishi, like to have contact with soil. When growing a species of this sort, you may want to bury the logs under the soil. Regardless of what you use to bury them, you'll be able to quickly tell when it's time to harvest as the mushrooms will grow upwards and outwards. Harvest when they are full size and then wait for the next flush. The particular species will determine how long your raft continues to produce, but you can expect several rich harvests at the minimum.

Outdoor Vegetable Beds: Just because we're talking about mushroom cultivation in this book doesn't mean that we can avoid vegetable gardening. If all you want to do is grow mushrooms, then you can just skip to the next section. But, if you already grow or are interested in growing vegetables, then you should know how well vegetable beds lend themselves to the addition of mushrooms. Crops that are mulched can have mushrooms, such as the wine cap, added to them with very little effort. But this isn't just about the mushrooms themselves. Rather, the mushrooms help out the growing environment.

You will need to stick to mushrooms that grow on mulch, so this means they're not a perfect fit for every kind of crop. But, if you are growing tomatoes or peppers, then you are probably already mulching the crop and wasting a great chance to increase your earnings come harvest. You can obviously sell the mushrooms to boost these earnings, but this isn't what I'm talking about. Plants and fungi have a symbiotic relationship. The mulch from the plants helps your mushrooms grow, but your mushrooms also help the growth of your plants. If you want to increase how much your crops yield, then adding mushrooms can be an easy way to achieve this. You end up with more vegetables to grow, as well as the new mushrooms you've harvested. Not only that, but adding mushrooms to your crops can greatly improve the quality of the soil.

Adding mushrooms to a garden bed is extremely easy, but you need to be extra-careful come that first harvest. We have less control over the bacteria and pathogens in the soil when compared to those crops we grow in isolation or indoors. Most of the time, this doesn't do us any harm. But we need to be careful when harvesting. You might have a batch of mushrooms that look like what you intended to grow, only to discover that something happened, and you are producing a species that isn't edible. When you start to see mushrooms popping in your garden beds, take one or two and run a spore print to make sure that it is the species you intended it to be. Of course, nine times out of ten, it will be. But you don't want to make an assumption and end up selling poisonous mushrooms to your customers. You won't have many return customers if you make a mistake like this.

MUSHROOM CULTIVATION

Indoor Methods: Indoor growing will typically cost more to start than outdoor growing does unless you are starting on a smaller scale. When the scale is small, indoor growing is the cheapest and quickest method. You can make indoor beds of the same size and design as your outdoor beds, but more often, indoor growers will use a combination of growing in containers, jars, or bags. There are also plenty of growers who design an indoor environment ideal for growing on rafts. Pretty much anything that can be done outdoors can be done indoors, but there are more options available to indoor growers in the long run.

These options come from the fundamental ability to control the indoor environment. We achieve this with heaters or AC units, fans, and humidifiers. These require funds for their initial purchase, and then more when the electricity bill comes. No matter how automated your setup is, it will still be up to you to check on the mushrooms and ensure they are growing healthily and show no signs of mold. Both of these point us towards the real essence of indoor cultivation: knowledge.

Without knowledge, indoor cultivation is doomed to fail. But a book like this can only take you so far and prepare you up to an extent. With all the theory in the world, you still need experience to become a master at mushroom cultivation. There is a higher cost to indoor cultivation, and it requires you to learn a lot more, but I am a firm believer in starting indoors, even if it is with just a tiny batch of oyster mushrooms. It has a higher barrier to entry, but if you can learn to cultivate mushrooms indoors, then you have a skill that can earn you money no matter where you are in the world. In the wilds, you know what mushrooms need to grow. With a house, you can always use the shed or backyard. But being able to grow mushrooms indoors means that you can make mushroom money from your studio apartment if it is all you have. As far as I am concerned, this is one of those skills which everybody should know because it can keep you from going hungry and help you earn a living.

MUSHROOM CULTIVATION

Grow Bags: The final growing method we'll look at is the grow bag. These take up far less space than rafts or garden beds do. You can also hang them closer together or in stacks of two or three, depending on the size. There isn't anything particularly special about a grow bag. They're just plastic bags with a port filter. The port filter is important because it allows for the fresh air that our mushrooms require to become nice and tasty. You can purchase grow bags that have been filled with substrate and sterilized already, though it isn't particularly hard to make your own.

Being extremely careful not to allow harmful bacteria to ruin the process, pack the bags full of the substrate used for growing. The filled bags are then placed in the pressure cooker for a couple of hours so that everything is properly sterilized. The bags should be sealed immediately and left to cool. Stick tape over the filter port. When the bags are fully cool, you have the perfect growing method for your mushrooms.

Introduce your mushroom spawn to the bag. This can be done by using a needle to inject it. You can puncture directly through the taped up port filter if you wish; however, it is faster to inject the bags at several places, so that the mycelium has a few starting positions, and can take over the bag much quicker. Tape is placed over any of the holes that you've made, and the bags are then left in the grow room. The lighting, temperature, and humidity levels will be set depending on the species being grown. The bags need to be checked to ensure they don't completely dry out. You can inject water into the bags if needed, just remember to tape up the hole afterward. Depending on what species you are growing, you could be harvesting in a matter of a few weeks. When grown in bags, it is crucial that you harvest the mushrooms when they are ready, as the bag is an environment that promotes rot and waste.

MUSHROOM CULTIVATION

Chapter Summary

- Different species require different cultivation methods to obtain the largest possible yields.

- Oyster mushrooms are found in Nature on trees that have fallen and collapsed. They like to be grown through the raft method as this uses logs such as they would find naturally. Moist logs can be cut open, inoculated, and then nailed shut and placed in a bag if desired. To grow oyster mushrooms using the raft method indoors will take up quite a bit of space in a grow room. Other methods can be used for indoor use if this space is not available.

- Shiitake mushrooms like to be grown on healthy hardwood logs. Logs are soaked, and holes are drilled all over. These holes are filled with mushroom spawn, and then sealed shut with wax. The ends of logs are also sealed with wax before being covered in plastic and left to develop. Shiitake mushrooms take a couple of months to begin fruiting. You can tell they are ready when you check them and see that the mycelium has entirely covered the ends of the log.

- Button mushrooms are grown on compost and manure, so they are a perfect fit for those cultivators who have a vegetable garden or livestock of their own. Button mushrooms are basically grown in a raised garden bed in the same way that most plants are. The mycelium is introduced with the right pH level and temperatures.

- Paddy straw mushrooms are grown on rice straw that has been wrapped up and kept in 18-inch bundles. They can be grown outside and are a staple of Chinese cuisine, which opens up the possibility of doing business with a Chinese restaurant if you choose to grow them.

- Outdoor garden beds are good fits for portobellos, wine caps, and inky caps. These mushrooms grow on fertilizer, and adding them to a crop can help to improve the overall health of the soil. It is best to grow in a raised bed garden, which requires a building material to create the sides. If you choose hardwood, then you can use the reishi species of mushroom. These mushrooms will grow from the wood of the raised garden bed, alongside mushrooms which grow from fertilizer inside the bed. These gardens need to be carefully placed, and they require a yard you can build them in, but they offer a great way to maximize the space and use it most effectively.

- Rafts are used to grow reishi, nameko, brick top, maitake, and pioppino mushrooms. These species like to grow on logs naturally, so rafts artificially create the environment necessary for growth. Logs are inoculated, which can take months. They are kept indoors in a controlled environment until the mycelium has totally spread throughout the logs. They are then taken outdoors and kept in an area that is shaded throughout the day and is quite damp. The soil is checked to make sure that it isn't

MUSHROOM CULTIVATION

full of heavy metals. A tarp is laid down if it is, and fresh soil is put on that. The fully inoculated logs are brought out, placed in the designated area, and covered in wood chips or other substrates as necessary for the species.

- Outdoor vegetable beds can benefit from having mushrooms added to them. The fungi will help to break down plant matter. Just make sure to take a spore print and confirm you've grown what you intended to.

- Indoor growing methods cost more money than outdoor methods do, but they offer a great level of control over the process.

- Grow bags are easy to use since they're filled with substrate that is then injected with mushroom spawn. Bags can easily be stacked to maximize the available space. It is important to check them often so that they never go dry.

In the next chapter, we will look at how to begin the growing process and get everything in place, sterilized, and mixed. We'll also look at the growing period as a whole, and when we need to move our mushrooms from one environment to another.

CHAPTER 6

GETTING STARTED WITH THE GROWING PROCESS

By this point, we have probably covered enough information for you to be able to grow your first few batches of mushrooms. But it has been spread out throughout the book. This chapter is going to do one thing and one thing only. We're going to go step-by-step through the process of growing your first mushrooms. Since it is the first, we're going to keep the costs as minimal as possible so that the barrier to entry is exceedingly low. Unfortunately, this also means that we aren't going to be covering the lab work.

While I am a strong proponent of cultivating your mushrooms from spore to plate, it definitely costs more time, money, and knowledge to pull this off. As beginners, our first batch of mushrooms will be grown from a mushroom spawn that we purchased from an online or local realtor. This is less than a kit; we're just purchasing the spawn itself. Speaking of which, we're going to stick to oyster mushrooms as recommended in Chapter Three, so it shouldn't be too hard to find a spawn. There are different types of oyster mushrooms that can be grown in the following method, but we'll be sticking to blue-grey oyster mushrooms as they are the easiest. They'll need to be kept between 50F and 68F, so make sure that you have a space that can be maintained at this temperature. Beyond this, you're just going to need a spray bottle and a kettle or pot for heating water. You will also require a bucket that can cope with water at boiling temperatures. That will basically serve as the pressure cooker in this method. A couple of plastic bags and some old cardboard, and you've got everything you need.

Step 1: Prepare the Growing Environment

Our substrate for growing in this approach is going to be the cardboard. We need to prepare the cardboard at this point because it is the physical growing environment that our oyster mushrooms are going to be living in. They are going to want to have a temperature no lower than 50F. Initially, they are going to need a place without light, and then, later on, they'll want a place with light. So you must prepare two different locations for your mushrooms, though you can simply make a note of the second location for use later. The first location should still have fresh airflow; therefore, be mindful of whether or not you need to introduce a fan to your setup.

You can grow mushrooms on cardboard without doing

anything, but the chances of the batch successfully making it to harvest is almost none. Without properly pasteurizing the cardboard first, we have an environment that's full of bacteria and other microorganisms. Since the conditions for mushroom growth is ideal for mold, we can lower our chances of failure and maximize those for our success by killing off all these possible threats right out of the gate.

First, cut your cardboard up into squares. That should make it easier to fit the cardboard into the container that holds your hot water, but we're also doing it in preparation for the inoculation step. Though speaking of that container, it's time to stuff all of your cardboard squared down into it. Use your pot or kettle to bring some water to a boil and pour it over the squares. You may need to boil more water since you don't want to stop until everything is fully submerged. Once it is, stick a top onto the container and let it sit. It'll take at least eight hours, but you can leave it be for longer while you go to sleep or head into work. You should be prepared to complete step two before you drain the bucket.

Step 2: Inoculate

This is the step during which you must be the most cautious. In a moment, you will have freshly pasteurized cardboard that is perfect for inoculation. But, if you are careless during this step, bacteria can get reintroduced back into the substrate, and step one will have been entirely for naught. You'll want to use gloves and thoroughly wash your hands. It might also be a good idea to lay out a clean plastic bag and open it up. That will make it easier to start laying the cardboard in a moment.

With cleanliness and setup out of the way, take your container of water and cardboard, and pour out as much water as you can. If you have a tight lid for the container, then open it a crack and pour, keeping one hand on the lid to prevent the pressure from knocking it loose. Once the majority of the water has drained, take the container back out to your work station. You are going to start layering the cardboard into the bag, but first, you need to ring it out a little. Take the first piece and squeeze the moisture out of it, being careful to keep it above the container so that it doesn't spill. Once you've squeezed out as much as you can, place the piece into the bag. This will act as the bottom foundation for this batch, so make sure you pick one of your larger pieces.

With the first piece laid out, next, you will open up the spawn that you purchased and spread some out over the cardboard. Take the next piece of cardboard, squeeze it dry, and place it in the bag to make a "spawn sandwich." Sprinkle some spawn on top of this one, and then grab the next piece. Repeat this until you are out of room in the bag, out of cardboard, out of bags, or out of spawn. To begin with, don't worry too much about getting the sizes right. It's a learning process, and how much cardboard you use will be determined by the size of your spawn and the size of your bags, so recommending a set amount is useless. Anything that isn't used in this first bag can be used for a second, and it's more than okay to have a bag that is only half-full.

When you have finished inoculating the bag, you can close it up. Some people keep this bag and move it; others will place it into a box to more easily transport it and catch any possible moisture that could spill. If you decide to go with shredded or stripped cardboard, then you will want to toss the cardboard into the bag, toss in the spawn, and mix it well. Make sure that you cut some slits into the sides of the bag, whether you use strips or squares. To properly trap carbon dioxide for mycelium growth, place your first bag into a second bag without any slits for air.

Step 3: Wait

The previous step required a considerable amount of caution, but this one requires almost nothing at all. Since you've already placed your cardboard directly into a bag, you just need to put it in a warm place. You already scouted out a place with a temperature of at least 50F in the first step, so you don't need to worry about deciding on where to put them here. Just use the one you already planned. Make sure that the bag is sealed before you tuck them away. You want the carbon dioxide to fill up in the bag at this stage.

Once you store the bag, wait a few days. Check on it after three or four days and make sure that it isn't leaking and that there is no water pooling up. If there is, drain this water. It is important to make a distinction between just being moist and collecting water. Water runs and pools at the bottom of the bag, moisture just stays diffused throughout the cardboard. If you have pools of water, it means that you didn't drain the cardboard as thoroughly as you should have. You should be careful when setting the bag to not place it on carpet or hardwood floors that could be damaged by excess water spill.

Once you have drained any excess water, close the bag and put it back into its space. Blue-grey oyster mushrooms will take a month to a month and a half before anything else needs to be done. They really don't need any help from you at this stage, and so you could go a month without looking at them without any issues. While you shouldn't

MUSHROOM CULTIVATION

forget about them, you need to try to at least a little bit. If you were to keep checking on them regularly, then you would be continually letting the carbon dioxide out. Instead, wait at least a month before checking on them.

To check, all you need to do is open the bag and look at the top layer. If the cardboard is covered completely with mycelia, then it is ready. If it looks like there is still some cardboard to go, then you should close the bag again and wait another week. Check it only once a week until it is ready. When the mycelium has finally overtaken the cardboard, the time is ripe for fruiting.

Step 4: Fruiting

When the mycelium is ready, it is up to us to make it start pinning. We do this by first opening up the bag. This releases the carbon dioxide that was trapped inside the bag, as well as lets fresh air in. The introduction of oxygen is what will begin the fruiting process that gives us our delicious mushrooms.

At this point, you will need that second location we mentioned in step one. If you haven't picked it out already, now is the time to do so. Keeping roughly the same temperature, you want to place your mushrooms in a space with some natural light. They don't need much. If you have enough light that you could read a book by, then you can grow mushrooms. From here, you need to tend to your mushrooms twice a day. Mushrooms will want to be sprayed twice a day. Once before bed, once in the morning. Use a spray bottle; don't just pour water onto them. When spraying, aim away from the walls of the bag. Do this by keeping the spray bottle level with the ground or pointed up. Never point the spray bottle down at your mushrooms. You should also spray the mushrooms themselves, and not the cardboard growing environment.

After two or three days, you'll see mushrooms begin to pin. As soon as you do, you can expect a harvest in the near future. They may take several weeks in step three, but they take next to no time here. Mushrooms are harvested by twisting them at the base of the stem. Use two fingers to take hold of the stem tightly, and then give a sharp twist to remove it.

If you continue to spray your mushrooms twice each day, you can expect a second harvest about two weeks later. The second harvest is generally of the same size as the first. Some batches will go for as many as five harvests, but there is an appreciable drop in size between them after the second. Eventually, it will stop producing mushrooms, and it can be tossed in the compost.

Step 5: What's Next?

The next step depends on you. If you still want to keep growing mushrooms, then you have exactly what you need. You can follow this guide again to produce another harvest, or you could use the mushrooms you just harvested to produce spores and create your own spawns. You may want to consider creating the necessary space and gathering the equipment needed to make a lab and grow room.

You'll have a delicious harvest of mushrooms. You can surely eat through a bunch of them, using many different recipes, or you can try to sell them locally. If you can't sell or eat them fast enough, you can preserve your mushrooms through several different methods for sale or consumption later on. In fact, we'll do precisely that in the next chapter.

MUSHROOM CULTIVATION

Chapter Summary

- This guide is for growing oyster mushrooms with the lowest initial investment possible.

- The first step in growing mushrooms is to prepare the growing environment.

- The growing environment is both the physical environment that you provide as a grow space, as well as the substrate that the mushrooms grow on.

- Blue-grey oyster mushrooms want a temperature no less than 50F, though they don't want light at this stage.

- Our substrate is old cardboard, so we first cut it into squares, and then stuff it into a bucket or container.

- We soak the cardboard in hot water by using a kettle or pot to bring the water to the boil and pouring it over the cardboard until it is entirely submerged. This kills off microorganisms that might compete for resources and destroy our mushroom crop.

- The cardboard is left to soak for at least eight hours.

- We need to be careful when emptying the water from our container. The cardboard is now safe, but if we aren't wary, then harmful organisms can sneak back onto it.

MUSHROOM CULTIVATION

- Pour out as much of the water as possible, and then squeeze the cardboard dry before using it.

- Take a sterilized plastic bag and place a piece of cardboard down. Pour some of your purchased mushroom spawn onto it. Put down another piece of cardboard and repeat the process until you are out of supplies.

- Close up the plastic bag and cut two slits in the sides for oxygen. Then, put this bag into another plastic bag and tie the outermost bag closed. This traps in CO_2 that helps the mycelium to grow.

- Your grow bag is placed somewhere dark with a temperature around 50F. After a couple of days, check on it to make sure there isn't water pooling up. Drain any that has and close the bag again.

- Leave the grow bag alone for the next month. Afterward, check it once a week by opening up the bag and seeing if the top layer of cardboard is covered in mycelium yet. If it isn't, close the bag and wait another week.

- When the mycelium has spread out fully, open up the bag. What that does is let the CO_2 out and oxygen in. The newly discovered oxygen tells your mushrooms that it is time to start fruiting.

- Within a couple of days, you will see your mushrooms pinning. It is a requirement that you keep them moist after opening the bag. Spray them with water twice a day.

- After pinning, you will have full-grown mushrooms in a few days.

- Harvest the mushrooms by grabbing them at the base and twisting them off rather than pulling them free.

- Continue to spray the grow bag with water twice a day, and you will have a second harvest in a few weeks. You may be able to get up to five harvests from a bag, though they will drop in size after the second one.

- With the mushrooms you have now harvested, you can use their spores to create your own spawns in the future.

In the next chapter, you will learn how to preserve your mushrooms after harvesting them so that you can keep them for a long time. The best part is that preserved mushrooms can still make you a lot of money, and there are even a few surprising ways you might not have considered before.

CHAPTER 7

PRESERVING MUSHROOMS

We'll be looking at selling our mushrooms in Chapter Nine, and we'll be covering recipes for cooking them in Chapter Ten. But, with the large size of mushroom harvests, you will find that you'll quickly need to learn how to preserve them. If you don't, then you are going to be letting a lot of mushrooms go to waste. There are five ways that we can preserve our mushrooms, though these can be broken down into three categories: freezing, pickling, drying.

We'll look at these methods by starting with the three ways of freezing our mushrooms. From there, we'll see how to dry out mushrooms and then how to pickle them. You may still be able to make money selling dried or pickled mushrooms, but the income will be much less than selling fresh. So, when it comes to preserving yours, go for which option you think tastes the best.

We will also take a look at how to take a spore print, which can be thought of as preserving the seeds of your mushrooms for later use or identification.

Freezing Mushrooms

To freeze mushrooms, they must first be blanched or cooked. This requires you to have a stove and a pot or pan. You'll also want to have a freezer bag or an airtight container. Frozen mushrooms will last nine to twelve months. We'll start by blanching our mushrooms. From there, we'll steam them, and then we'll fry them.

Blanching: Begin by washing your mushrooms. Remember that mushrooms should only be washed prior to cooking or blanching. If you wash them after they are harvested, this will promote faster rotting. However, we need to make sure they are clean before blanching them, so wash them under cool water. Also, give them a quick clean with your hands to wipe any dirt away.

Next, take your large pot and fill it with water. Add a little bit of salt. There is an old wives' tale that adding salt to a pot makes it boil faster. This isn't true, but it will help your mushrooms to keep their flavor better. A lid isn't necessary, but it can help to speed up the process.

As the water is heating, cut the mushrooms. You can do slices or chunks, but it will be much easier to preserve them when they have already been cut. Just make sure that you cut them all roughly the same size. Don't go from chunks to slices for the same batch.

When the water is boiling, it will be time to dunk the mushrooms. But it only takes two minutes to blanch them. Since there isn't much time during the blanching process itself, you might like to prepare the aftercare materials first. Take a bowl and fill it with cold water and ice cubes. This needs to stay cold. We'll use it to cool down our mushrooms in a few moments. Try to have enough water to cover all of the mushrooms, but you can always add more if there wasn't enough.

With the water boiling, toss your prepared mushrooms into the boiling water and use a cooking utensil to make sure that they are all in the water. Cook the mushrooms for two minutes, and then take them off the heat and dump them into a colander. Give the colander a good shake to let excess moisture roll off. Quickly drop the colander into the ice water. If the water is not fully covering the mushrooms, then add some more, making sure it is cold. The mushrooms should be cold in a few minutes, no more than five. Immediately put them into the containers or bags that you have ready. Mushrooms get larger as they freeze, so don't pack them too tightly. Stick the mushrooms into the freezer and they can keep for a year. It is best to keep them deep in the freezer. The front of the freezer around the door experiences lots of temperature change when the door is opened while the back holds onto its chill much longer.

Steaming: Steamed mushrooms are a delicacy that fires up the taste buds and makes your mouth water. But learning how to steam your mushrooms is a significant part of learning how to freeze them. It offers a different approach than blanching, one which holds onto a much higher quality of flavor. It shares this with the fry and freeze method.

To begin, wash your mushrooms. Remember to clean them only before cooking, not days or even hours in advance. Wash them thoroughly and while they are still whole before you cut them. Even though we will be removing bits from them, wash them before you cut them so that dirt and germs don't get into the openings. When they have been cleaned and dried off, take them over to your cutting board. Remove the stem as close to the cap as you can without cutting into the cap. Flip the stemless mushroom onto the cap and slice it into quarters. With steaming, we always stick with quarters when we are planning to freeze them. When you are dealing with a lot of mushrooms, it is useful to pick a size of cut and make it exclusive to a single approach. Going with quarters for steamed or fried mushrooms, we can stick with slices for blanching. Doing that will make it easier to tell the difference between the various mushrooms we've frozen.

We added a dash of salt to our water when blanching mushrooms. That's done to help preserve their flavor, as well as keeping their color instead of allowing them to darken. When it comes to steaming, we add another step to the process. Add two cups of water to a bowl or pot large enough to fit all of your quartered mushrooms. If two cups aren't enough to fully cover your mushrooms, then use four cups. Stick to multiples of two. Add a teaspoon of lemon juice for every two cups of water you've used. Add your mushrooms and give them five minutes to soak up the liquid. This isn't necessary if you don't care about their color, but aesthetics are an important part of cooking, so I recommend taking the extra five minutes to do so.

Next, it is time to steam the mushrooms at last. You will need a stovetop steamer for this. A rice cooker with a steaming option may do the trick for small batches, but a larger stovetop steamer is necessary if you have anything beyond a single, small batch. Plus, a stovetop steamer is a great addition to any kitchen, so getting one should be a must for everyone, regardless of whether or not they're even growing mushrooms. The size of your steamer will determine how much water you use, but most work the same way. Put some water in the bottom of the pot, add your steaming tray, and fill it up full of mushrooms. Put a lid over the pot and wait. It shouldn't take any longer than five minutes. In fact, it often takes less time. You can tell a mushroom has been properly steamed by stabbing it with a fork. It should take very little effort to poke the fork through all but the center of your mushroom quarter. The smaller your mushrooms are, the less time it takes to steam. You could steam whole mushrooms if you wanted; I would recommend doing this if you are steaming to freeze. If you are steaming to eat, then I highly recommend trying whole steamed mushrooms that you've grown yourself; it is a delicious and rewarding experience.

As you take out the steaming tray, give it one or two shakes to knock free any excess moisture. Using freezer bags, trays, or whatever other containers you have prepared, simply fill them up with your steamed mushrooms. As previously mentioned, frozen mushrooms expand, so you will need to leave a little bit of space in the container to prevent this from damaging them. When you have filled the containers, let them sit out for a bit to cool down. That should only take thirty to sixty minutes; this gives you enough time to prepare another batch, take a shower, watch a show, or prepare dinner. You don't need to pay the mushrooms any attention during this stage; you just want to make sure that they aren't going into the freezer hot. This is less to do with your mushrooms and more to do with the other items in your freezer. Tossing in items that are still hot raises the overall temperature inside the freezer, and this can cause issues with other foods thawing out, such as your freshly blanched mushrooms. Many foods can only be frozen once, as thawing them out and freezing them again allows for the growth of harmful bacteria and rot.

As with blanched mushrooms, you can store steamed mushrooms for about a year. Remember to keep them near the back of your freezer. If you have never cleaned or considered the organization of your freezer, then now is an ideal time to start. Items that are used quickly should be near the front, and those that are kept for any length of time should be pushed to the back. Five minutes of cleaning your freezer can help you keep your food healthy and ready to eat for months.

MUSHROOM CULTIVATION

Frying: The final approach to freezing is the fry and freeze. Fried mushrooms are among my favorite foods to eat, so I feel comfortable telling you that this is my favorite approach to freezing. Being able to add fried mushrooms to my pizzas and soups is a major time saver. Unfortunately, I will also admit that frying definitely has one glaring weakness that blanching and steaming don't. Whereas mushrooms that have been blanched or steamed are able to keep for roughly a year, fried mushrooms only keep for about three quarters of a year or nine months. Because of this, I recommend frying and freezing should be carried out less often. I like to freeze a big batch of fried mushrooms and wait until I have used them all up before I do a second. I usually end up with two or three freezer bags filled with fried mushrooms, and I tend to use them up in four or five months.

To begin with, wash and clean your mushrooms. At this point, you already know how this is done. When cutting, I like going with quarters for my fried mushrooms. This can make it harder to tell your fried mushrooms from your steamed mushrooms, but I leave myself an evident sign by leaving the stems on my mushrooms before frying them. If you aren't a fan of the stems, then it doesn't hurt you to remove them. If you are a fan, you may want to remove them, fry and freeze them specifically. The best indicator for this is personal taste, so use your preferences to guide your decision.

There aren't as many steps to frying mushrooms as there are with the other ways of freezing. Get yourself a frying pan that comfortably fits your mushrooms and toss a little butter or oil into it. Let it heat up and melt the butter or loosen up the oil. Once the pan is fully heated, and your butter entirely melted, toss the mushrooms in. It only takes a couple of minutes to fry up your mushrooms. Smaller species may take only two minutes, larger ones may take up to five, but most quarters will be good with about three minutes of cooking. Mushrooms need to be stirred a little while cooking, but you want to avoid over-stirring. Once a minute or so should be fine. If you like your mushrooms to be spiced, then now is the time to add some. I personally enjoy a dash of basil, but you can use anything you like.

As your mushrooms fry, you'll see them turning brown. You can tell they're ready when they've turned brown all over. Keep in mind that the caps will be a darker shade of brown than the stems are. You want the caps to be an even color and the stems to be an even color, but these two colors don't need to be the same. Focus on making sure that each part of the mushroom is even to the equivalent parts on the other pieces. This way, you don't burn your mushrooms by trying to get the stems as dark as the caps. When they're done, take them off the stove and scoop them onto a plate to cool. You'll notice that there isn't a lot of moisture left in the pan at this stage. If there is, then you'll want to give them another minute on the heat.

When they've cooled down, pour them into your freezer bags or containers and toss them into the freezer. You now have fried mushrooms, seasoned to taste and ready to be stored for three quarters of a year. You can tell when any of your frozen mushrooms have gone bad because they'll start to become slimy and tender, and new substances will start to grow on them. If you open up the container and find slimy mushrooms, just throw them out. It's never worth gambling on mushrooms once they've started to go bad.

Drying Your Mushrooms

Dried mushrooms are great in soups, stews, and sauces. As a preservation technique, drying works especially well because the mushrooms are able to keep their flavor without any problems. With the freezing techniques, we can preserve some of the flavor by adding steps to the process to compensate for the natural loss of flavor that happens when cooking. With drying, so long as we don't use too high a temperature, the mushrooms taste the most like they would when fresh. While there are many approaches you can take to drying, we will be using a dehydrator. This electronic kitchen appliance will make drying your mushrooms easy. You can also use a dehydrator for making your own jerky or granola, as well as sun-dried tomatoes, dehydrated fruits, and potpourri. If you are considering drying mushrooms, then this approach is the most rapid there is, and it gives you so many other delicious options. A dehydrator ranges from $50 to $400, depending on the size and complexity of the machine.

MUSHROOM CULTIVATION

Plug in your dehydrator and set it for a temp of 110F. Most dehydrators are slow to warm up, so you can expect this to take anywhere from two or three hours to upwards of eight or nine. You can use a higher heat for less time drying (though it'll take longer to heat up), but I don't recommend it. The higher the heat, the more flavor that is lost in the process. Wait until the dehydrator is heated, or very close to being heated, before you wash your mushrooms.

After washing, you are going to want to be very careful

when slicing them. How thick they are is going to determine how long they take to dry. It is recommended that you slice them as thin as you can, but this is simply to make the drying process quicker. It is more important to make sure that they are sliced the same thickness rather than the thinnest one. This is done so that the pieces all dry evenly. If you have thick slices next to thin slices, then you should check on the thin ones and remove them before the larger ones finish. You can, of course, dry both together in the same batch, but it will take much more effort on your part when compared to a batch that has been evenly sliced.

A dehydrator is made up of threaded trays that allow the heated air to pass through the whole appliance. Lay your slices out on the tray so that they are flat. If you do have slices that have been cut to a different size, then you can make your life a little bit easier by keeping them to the same tray. Place the larger slices on the bottom tray, with each subsequent tray having thinner and thinner slices. That way, you can check on the top tray and remove it when it is done, making it easier to check on the slices that should be ready next. At the bare minimum, you can expect the drying process to take three hours. Go and take a walk or grab a nap, but if it's the latter, set a timer to remind yourself to check on them.

To check on them, simply open up the dehydrator and see if they are ready. It is quite easy to tell when a mushroom has been dehydrated fully. Pick it up, being careful not to burn yourself. Right away, it should feel different from the mushroom slice that went in. If you can snap it in half like a fortune cookie, then you know that it's definitely ready. Remove any that are done. Those that aren't can be left for another hour. Check on them again and remove them if they are ready. If they aren't, then go ahead and wait another hour, repeating the process until they are finally done. You expect most species to finish in three to five hours, but there are some that need longer. You should never leave a dehydrator on overnight, so try to schedule your drying sessions to begin before noon.

As the mushrooms are removed from the dehydrator, they are set aside to cool off. It typically takes an hour or so. You can start to package them once they are dry, or you can wait for the rest of the batch in the dehydrator to finish. If you have taken out all of the mushrooms from the dehydrator, I want to suggest that you leave it plugged in and turned on still. You might notice after they've cooled down that a few slices aren't fully dried. If you've left the dehydrator on, then it is easy to put them back in for a little while to finish up the job. If you unplug the dehydrator, it's going to take a few hours until it is back up to temperature.

Dried mushrooms can be stored in airtight containers such as sealed bags or jars. They are stored on a shelf, but it should be one that is in a dark and cool location. A basement or cellar pantry is an ideal place for dried mushrooms. Given the right conditions, they'll keep for six to twelve months. When you want to use them again, it is easy to toss dried mushrooms into a meal. But if you put them into a bowl and pour some boiling water onto them to sit, they will rehydrate after a half-hour bath. Make sure that you only rehydrate mushrooms you plan on using. You won't be able to preserve them any further at this point. Keep in mind, too, that dried mushrooms go bad differently than frozen mushrooms do. Frozen mushrooms start to get slimy and gross. Dried mushrooms don't really look much different when they go bad, but they do smell different. In fact, they smell different because they don't smell at all. That rich aroma that mushrooms have eventually fades away. If your dried mushrooms don't have a smell, then throw them out.

Pickling Your Mushrooms

Pickling your mushrooms isn't a fantastic way to preserve them for the long term, as they only keep about a month when done quickly. But pickling does offer another way of enjoying them and increasing their longevity when compared to fresh mushrooms. It also brings us to our more interesting approaches to keeping mushrooms. We'll be focusing on pickling, but other ways that we can increase our mushrooms are by mixing them into sauces or salsas. These offer us more goods to sell at farmers' markets or local grocery stores. They also give us a wider variety of flavors to go with our meals. As much as I love fried mushrooms, it would get pretty tiresome eating them all the time without switching things up. Pickling and creating sauces offer this much-needed spice of life.

I'm sure that you can guess the first step here. That's right; we have to wash our mushrooms and cut them if we so choose. This is up to taste, although size also plays a role. Smaller mushrooms should be kept whole in general. Larger mushrooms might need to be cut to fit into the jars without issue. After cleaning and cutting, you should prepare the pickling jar. That is done before cooking so that it is easy to transfer the mushrooms into it. You want to go with a jar made out of thick glass, as it is going to have hot pickling juice poured in before it is shoved in the fridge. Going from room temperature to burning hot and back down to cold is very stressful on glass, and a thinner jar runs the risk of cracking and making an awful mess. You may want to add some herbs such as oregano, dill, or bay leaves. That's a matter for individual taste, and I encourage you to experiment with different combinations to find your favorites. Leave the lid off the jar for the time being, though it is a good idea to test and make sure that it creates an airtight seal. Testing the lid at this stage will prevent a headache later in the process.

Next, we need to make the pickling solution. You'll want a large saucepan for this one. Emphasize height over width when picking a pan. You will want a minimum of three quarters a cup of water and one third a cup of white vinegar. We will focus on the ingredients for a baseline mixture. Vinegar has a reaction with certain metals, and the mixture will take on a metallic flavor if you use one of these. Use a ceramic, glass, or stainless steel saucepan for this mixture to avoid this flavor. Of course, if you actually enjoy a bit of a metallic taste, then you may purposefully want to use cast iron or copper here.

Add a tablespoon of salt and another of black peppercorns. These will give you the base spices needed for the pickling brine. At this point, you may want to add in other spices such as mustard seed or cajun spice. Don't forget that the flavors from the brine will be combined with the herbs in the jar. You may love the taste of rosemary with mushrooms, but when you add rosemary to the brine and to the jar, it can become overpowering.

After your spices, toss in your mushrooms and turn the heat on. You can keep it at a medium temperature. Wait until the water begins to boil. Smaller mushrooms will only need a minute or two; larger mushrooms will take upwards of five. You'll want to try to avoid overcooking, as this can result in a mushy and slightly disagreeable end product. After cooking at a boil, reduce the heat down to a simmer. Make sure that you don't keep boiling your mushrooms. You want to simmer them for fifteen minutes, but if the water is still boiling, then you are going to end up ruining them by keeping them in that long.

When the time has elapsed, take the saucepan off the stove. Use a spoon or spatula to scoop out the mushrooms and drop them into your jar. Get all of the pieces transferred first. Then, being careful not to burn yourself, lift the saucepan, and carefully pour the liquid brine into the jar until it's full. Tightly screw the lid on. Wait for the jar to cool off, and you have yourself some pickled mushrooms to store in the fridge. You will want to give them three or four days to settle before enjoying them. Remember to eat them quickly, as they only keep for a month.

Preserving Spore Prints

After you have grown your mushrooms, you may want to take a spore print from them for later use. The primary purpose of a spore print is as a diagnostic tool for identifying the species of mushroom you are holding. If you decide to collect mushrooms in the wild, you will become intimately familiar with spore prints because they're necessary to keep you alive. There are plenty of mushrooms that look similar to each other, except for the fact that they are poisonous. You might not be able to tell two species apart from each other through eyesight alone. But, if you take a spore print, you can see exactly what species you are dealing with. In this manner, spore prints are like the fingerprints of the mushroom kingdom.

When you grow mushrooms, it is a smart idea to have a print of the species you are looking to grow. This is especially true when growing outdoors, as there is more room for Nature's chaos to work. After your mushrooms begin to grow, harvest one and take a spore print first. If you already have a preserved spore print from the intended species, then you can compare it against the new one. If you haven't, don't worry. There are tons of online resources available such as First-nature.com, or you can purchase spore prints from a site like Mushrooms.com. These offer easy ways to get your hands on some prints to ensure that you are working only with the species you actually intended to. Many growers, myself included, recommend taking a spore print after every first harvest. In time, this will give you a spore library that will come in handy. It may even save your life by warning you that the mushroom you hold isn't what you think it is.

Taking a spore print changes depending on the way the

mushroom is shaped. The two most common varieties are those with gills or pores. There are other mushrooms that have even more unique physiologies, but we'll be sticking with gills and pores for the time being. To take a spore print from a mushroom with gills, you need to remove the stem and press the cap, gills on the button, onto a piece of paper. Since the spores are on the surface of the gill, pressing it down is all it takes. You may want to sprinkle a single drop of water onto the top of the cap, as this will help to loosen up the spores. It takes anywhere from a couple of hours to a full day for the spores to all fall and create the print, so you can set it up and leave it by itself. Just make sure to put a glass or a bowl or something protective over the cap to prevent it from being jostled or getting contaminated with dust and dirt. If the mushroom has pores instead of gills, then, in general, you need to follow the same procedure. The only real issue is the fact that mushrooms with pores are often much tougher, and this makes them harder to get spores from. To make it easier, take some paper towel and wet it so that it is damp. Wrap the mushroom in the wet paper towel, and leave it alone for eight hours. It should be soft enough to take a spore print afterward. Remember, though, that the moisture will cause the mushroom to begin rotting much sooner than it usually would. As a rule, you will be throwing away the mushrooms you made the spore print with rather than cooking and eating them.

A spore print can be sprayed with a little hair spray or artist spray in order to be preserved for long term collecting. These prints can last upwards of twenty years if properly cared for with a minimal amount of handling. Instead of using the spore of your mushroom print for further cultivation, you should store the print, and use fresh spores from the remaining mushrooms you've harvested. You can begin cultivating a new batch from a spore print. We often do this when we are first starting work with a new species, and want to begin the cultivation process from scratch rather than buying a premade spawn. But, when you have access to fresh spores, save your prints and make use of the resources you have in high supply.

MUSHROOM CULTIVATION

Chapter Summary

- If you don't sell or eat your mushrooms fast enough, you will need to know how to preserve them to keep them from going to waste. We can preserve information about our mushrooms, too, but we do this through a spore print.

- We can freeze mushrooms, dry them, or pickle them and turn them into sauces.

- Freezing mushrooms gives us three of our five preservation methods: Blanching, frying, and steaming.

- Frozen mushrooms will keep for up to a year.

- To blanch mushrooms: Wash the mushrooms, cut them into chunks or slices that are all roughly the same size. Bring a pot of water to boil with a pinch of salt in it. When the water is boiling, put in your cut mushrooms and cook them for two minutes. Take the mushrooms out and put them in a colander. Dunk the colander into a bowl of ice water to cool the mushrooms off quickly. Let them sit for a few minutes. Take the mushrooms out of the ice water, package them in freezer containers, and put them in the freezer.

- To steam mushrooms: Wash the mushrooms, cut them into evenly-sized pieces, and remove the stems. Mix two cups of water and a teaspoon of lemon juice. Let the mushrooms soak in this mixture for five minutes, then toss them in the steamer for five minutes. Take the mushrooms out of the steamer and remove any excess moisture. Put mushrooms into freezer containers and then store.

- To fry mushrooms: Wash mushrooms and cut them evenly. Stems can be left on. Melt butter in a pan and toss in mushrooms. Fry them for up to five minutes. Add spices to taste. Once they are brown, remove from heat, and let them cool down. When fully cool, toss into containers and store in the freezer.

- Store frozen mushrooms in the back of the freezer away from the door.

- Dried mushrooms can be sold to chefs for use in soups and stews. They are dried using a dehydrator set for 110F. It takes most dehydrators several hours to get to this temperature. It is best not to go any hotter, as higher temperatures will cause flavor to be lost. Mushrooms are cleaned and cut into even-sized pieces. There are several trays, and so pieces can be grouped by size to narrow down the variance. Mushrooms are left in the dehydrator for several hours before they are removed and left to cool. Dried mushrooms can be snapped when bent sharply. They are stored in airtight containers in cool, dark locations. They keep for about a year and should be thrown out when they lose their smell.

- Pickling mushrooms will keep them good for a month, as well as offer you new flavors and a new product to sell.

MUSHROOM CULTIVATION

- Mushrooms are pickled by being cooked in a brine. Mushrooms are washed, but they don't have to be cut if they are small. A jar is kept nearby and filled with any spices you desire. The jar will go from being very hot to very cold quickly, so only use thick glass.

- To make the pickling bring, add three-quarters of a cup of water with one-third a cup of white vinegar. Add a tablespoon of salt and a tablespoon of black peppercorns. Add any other spices you want here. Toss in the mushrooms and bring the whole thing to a boil. Reduce heat and simmer for fifteen minutes. At the end, scoop the mushrooms into the jar, and then fill up the remaining space with liquid. Put the jar into the fridge. It'll take three days before it is done, but you now have yourself some pickled mushrooms.

- Spore prints are taken so as to get an accurate analysis of the mushrooms you are growing. When you are growing a mushroom, you should always take a spore print and compare it to the expected spore print before you eat or sell them. Some species look alike, but a spore print is like a fingerprint, each species has one that is unique and tells us precisely what we have grown.

- Spore prints are done differently depending on where the spores of that particular species are located. In general, we remove the stem and put the mushroom cap onto a white paper. A drop of water is dripped onto the top of the cap to knock the spores loose. This is left to sit for the night. The spores will be knocked free, and they'll create a spore print on the paper. This is then sprayed with hair spray or artist spray in order to stick to the paper.

- Learn how to take and preserve spore prints. You should make taking a spore print a part of every single harvest. It might slow down the harvest by a day, but it can save your life. Mushrooms can potentially be deadly. Taking a spore print is how you ensure that you never accidentally eat or sell contaminated mushrooms to your customers.

In the next chapter, you will learn all about fungi. While all mushrooms are fungi, not every fungus is a mushroom. We'll take a look at the different types of fungi, how they go about reproducing, and where you can find them out in the world.

CHAPTER 8

UNDERSTANDING FUNGI

When discussing mushrooms or reading about them, you will see that they are a form of fungi. However, they are far from the only type of fungi. Fungi are one of the more important organisms on our planet. Fungi are responsible for breaking down dead plant matter. They break down dead trees so that they can go back into the soil and the environment. Since it is fungi that break down compost, it might come as no surprise to realize that it is fungi that create the nutrients we want in our soil. Without fungi, the nutrients wouldn't be present, and our crops would starve. There are also different types of fungi that help sheep and other animals to digest grass. So without fungi, there are whole species that wouldn't be able to eat enough to stay healthy.

But what are fungi?

Fungi are an entire kingdom unto themselves. We have the animal kingdom with its abundant life forms. There is the plant kingdom, that makes up the largest of Earth's kingdoms. For many years, fungi were regarded as a part of this plant kingdom. But it turns out that fungi aren't plants at all. It was thought that fungi simply grow, and therefore, acts like a plant. But there are some kinds of fungi that are able to move around during certain life stages. Fungi also don't need to get energy from the sun or CO_2. This takes them out of the plant kingdom, but it doesn't make them animals. They actually eat like animals, in that they break down what they eat to absorb energy, but they are too plant-like to be called animals. Thus, fungi became their own realm.

In this chapter, we'll briefly talk about the different types of fungi, their characteristics, how they reproduce, and where you can find them. Remember that we aren't talking about mushrooms here, but the broader category in which mushrooms fall into.

Types of Fungi

There are more than forty different families of fungi. These range from being extremely different from one another, to being as similar as crocodiles and alligators. To look at each type would become exceedingly boring, as some differences are so minor that you need to look at the DNA makeup of the fungi to spot it. You can get a clear understanding of the different fungi by choosing a handful of these to explore. This allows the conversation to stay both focused and expansive enough, without being bogged down by scientific jargon that doesn't matter to the lay mushroom cultivator.

Mushroom cultivators are well acquainted with Basidiomycota. This is the family that mushrooms come from. Sometimes referred to as the family of mushrooms and toadstools, this is a bit redundant. There is no difference between a toadstool and a mushroom on a scientific scale. These names are just used to denote whether or not a mushroom is edible. If it is poisonous, then it is called a toadstool. This is a causal definition, not a scientific one. The Basidiomycota family is the tastiest of the various types of fungi, but it is hardly the most practical one.

MUSHROOM CULTIVATION

Less practical still are those fungi in the microsporidia family. As the prefix "micro-" suggests, these are tiny little fungi. In fact, they are only a single cell. This makes them among the smallest microorganisms on the planet. Yet, despite their size, they can be quite deadly. They are primarily found to infect beetles, but there are cases in which microsporidia have been responsible for human illness. A healthy person is unlikely to be sickened by microsporidia, but those that are immunocompromised can face considerable risk from infection.

While most mushrooms are Basidiomycota, the rare morel mushroom is part of the Ascomycota family. Yet this family is among the most practical, useful, and essential organisms to ever thrive on this planet. It is from Ascomycota fungi that we discovered penicillin and set the stage for modern medicine. If it weren't for fungi, we wouldn't have nearly as many effective and lifesaving medical breakthroughs as we've had over the last century.

We'll finish out with a look at the different types of fungi by examining Neocallimastigomycota and Blastocladiomycota. The first, Neocallimastigomycota, is one of the hardest words to pronounce. Don't worry if you can't; you won't have to deal with this fungus much because it lives inside plant-eating animals. These fungi break down grass and other plant materials and turn them into carbohydrates for the animal to use as energy. Neocallimastigomycota is often grouped with Blastocladiomycota as they are "farmer's fungi." Where Neocallimastigomycota lives inside livestock,

Blastocladiomycota lives inside the soil. This fungus absorbs dead plant matter and other waste before producing the nutrients necessary for plants to flourish in the soil. If it weren't for these two fungi working together, farming and growing our food would be impossible.

Fungi Characteristics

Fungi are interesting organisms. They are eukaryotic. This refers to their structure and the fact that their cells have a proper nucleus. They don't have a vascular system, and so there are no pathways to carry blood or blood-like substances. They don't go through photosynthesis, nor do they turn green due to sunlight. They have cell walls like plants do, but they absorb energy through digestion like animals. We'll be speaking more about reproduction in a moment, but we've already encountered the process. All fungi reproduce through spores, though there are different types. They can't move, or so we once thought. We know that there are some fungi that can move during the reproduction process. But, beyond this stage, there is no movement. They don't have roots or leaves like plants, and they can grow in any direction. One of the intriguing features of this growth in any direction is that it can be down or throughout a substrate. With plants, you don't expect to see a rose grow inside of the dirt, apart from its roots. But fungi can grow all through the dirt, with each part being pretty much the same.

Fungi are among the most fascinating organisms on the

planet. There has continued to be new and exciting research conducted on them to this day. One recent study found that fungi, primarily mycelium, create a vast web beneath the soil of forests. Mycelium connects all of the trees together and creates a system through which biological information can be sent. This helps all of the trees in the forest to share their nutrients and warnings about illnesses and pests. Almost like a biological version of the internet, I can't resist titling this as the Wood Wide Web. With discoveries as profound as this being discovered all the time, there are still going to be many characteristics of fungi left for us to discover. What there is already is mind-boggling.

Reproduction of Fungi

Fungi have two forms of reproduction. The first is asexual reproduction. This happens with a single "parent." Sexual reproduction requires two parents for it to happen. Interestingly, most fungi can reproduce sexually. Being humans, we almost instinctively feel the need to ask why we'd ever bother reproducing asexually if we didn't have to.

Fungi, on the other hand, simply wants to produce as fast as possible. To do so, asexual reproduction is the way to go. It happens quicker, and it creates more offspring. It suffers in that asexual reproduction creates genetically identical offspring. If there is a problem in the fungus's genetics, then it is passed on just the same as the desirable parts. One of the ways this reproduction is accomplished is through the creation and release of spores. Spores don't always produce offspring, but they can achieve asexual reproduction in this manner. When a part of a fungus breaks off from the rest, it can continue to grow. A piece of one organism splits off, and it results in two organisms. If a piece of mycelium breaks off, prior to the fruiting body of the fungi growing, then it is called fragmentation. This also results in a genetically identical organism budding, but it just happens earlier in the growth cycle.

Sexual reproduction is performed for the genes of both parents to be combined. Just as with humans, this creates a larger gene pool and prevents biological errors from occurring. But sexual reproduction by fungi isn't anything like human reproduction. Spores grow little leg-like protrusions that then connect and join with the protrusions from another fungus's spores. The nuclei from these two different spores combine and become one. From there, new fungi can grow. It will show more genetic diversity. It is possible to combine and create particular strains of fungi, as genetic information is carried to subsequent generations. While this is far beyond a beginner, it does suggest intriguing opportunities for mushroom cultivators and scientists the world over.

MUSHROOM CULTIVATION

Where to Find Fungi?

Fungi can grow in all sorts of different places. Molds are the most typical, as anyone with a fridge or a leaky shower head knows. Fungi like to grow on biological substances. Wet and damp wood, rotting food, the soil, under the front deck. If you go into your backyard and start turning rocks over and looking at the base of your trees, you will quickly find dozens of places where fungi are growing.

Because there is so much of the stuff and it grows on such a variety of substances, it is pretty much everywhere. But it isn't entirely everywhere. You don't find it on metal unless it is close to the ground. It also tends to be averse to those bright patches that get full sunlight all day. But anywhere dark, damp, or dank is a place where fungi love to grow. You can make use of this knowledge by educating yourself on the growing habits and the appearance of certain varieties. If you have a woodpile that you want to rot faster, you could try going into the woods and looking for some wood-decay fungus such as brown rot. There are many uses for fungi, and they can be quite easy to find and identify. If you are looking for more ways to learn about mushrooms and fungi, your best bet may just be going for a hike through the woods.

Chapter Summary

- All mushrooms are fungi. Not every fungus is a mushroom.

- Fungi are one of the most important organisms on the planet. They help to keep soil healthy, keep our livestock healthy, and they do a pretty good job of keeping us healthy. Different kinds are at work in each of these examples, but the end result is still one vital and impressive organism.

- Fungi were, at one time, thought to be part of the plant kingdom, but recent discoveries have led to them being classified as their own kingdom of living organisms alongside the plant kingdom and our animal kingdom.

- There are more than forty kinds of fungi. Some are similar. Many are as far apart as two species from the same family can be.

- Mushrooms and toadstools are most often from the Basidiomycota family.

- Toadstools and mushrooms are the same things on a scientific level, but the title toadstool is usually applied to a poisonous mushroom.

- The Ascomycota family of fungi also produces mushrooms, but it is far more important than the Basidiomycota family. This is due to the Ascomycota family being the family in which penicillin was discovered.

- The microsporidia family is composed of single-celled fungi that can cause infections and health complications in the body. Most often, it affects insects such as beetles, but an immunocompromised individual may face health complications if exposed to microsporidia.

- Neocallimastigomycota is one of our two farming fungi. Living inside the stomach of livestock, it breaks down plant matter so that it can be converted into carbohydrates.

- The other farming fungi is Blastocladiomycota. This particular type lives in the soil and breaks down dead plant matter to turn it into nutrients.

- Fungi have cell walls like plants, but they digest food like animals. They produce through spores or cloning, don't need the sunlight, and they don't move once developed.

- Research continues to be conducted on fungi, and some of these discoveries are on the cutting edge of scientific knowledge.

- Fungi can reproduce asexually or sexually. Asexual reproduction is managed at times through the spreading of spores, but these require specific circumstances to grow. More often, asexual reproduction is achieved in the wild through fragmentation of the mycelium or by pieces budding off.

- Sexual reproduction is achieved when the spores of two different species come together to form a single nucleus. Sexual reproduction of fungi can produce fungi with new genetic qualities. Future generations will keep the newly-gained traits.

- Fungi are found anywhere that is dark, damp, and cool. They can be found under your decks, on the backside of rocks, and all over the rotting food in the back of your fridge. Finding fungi is easy as can be, and learning how to identify fungi can give you access to a new tool that can make gardening easier.

In the next chapter, you will learn how to earn a profit from your gourmet mushrooms. From selling them at the farmers' market, to drying and preserving them, or selling them to local stores, there are always plenty of ways to earn a dollar from your mushrooms.

CHAPTER 9

PROFITING FROM GOURMET MUSHROOMS

In Chapter One, we looked at how you may approach a restaurant to sell your gourmet mushrooms. That certainly isn't the only approach, though. In this chapter, we're going to take a look at a few more ways that you can profit from your mushrooms. Grocery stores, markets, and alternative products are all highly useful outlets when it comes to increasing our mushroom money.

Grocery Stores

If you can get a contract in place with a local grocery store, then it will be easy to sell your harvests when they come in. But if you want to make the biggest profit possible, then you will need to be careful about which store you approach. Approaching a store itself is quite easy, though. Just call up and ask them if they buy local products from farmers and cultivators. There's every chance they will be happy to walk you through their onboarding process.

But picking the right store requires a little consideration. The thing to remember is that we are selling gourmet mushrooms. A grocery store without much variety of mushrooms isn't going to be able to sell gourmet mushrooms at full value. Without the customers, there is no demand, and your product will end up going to waste. Rather than calling the first grocery store in your area, go online and see if there are any higher-end grocers in the area. These are more likely to be interested in exclusive products and will cater to gourmet tastes. That results in more mushrooms being sold at a higher price. If they are grown to quality, then there will be a demand for them to fill in these stores.

Farmers' Markets

Farmers' markets are one of the best places for selling your harvests. They often bring out lots of people, people specifically looking for organic and healthy alternatives to the chemically produced crops of large corporations. It is unfortunate that they tend to be closed down during the winter months, though there are some indoor farmers' markets that continue throughout the year. These tend to survive through the sale of preserved products, which we'll discuss in a moment, as well as arts and crafts. If you grow your gourmet mushrooms indoors with a carefully controlled environment, then you can continue to grow in the winter and produce crops when there is little fresh food competition.

Farmers' markets require you to attend the event. Most will require you to pay a fee for your table, with the more ideal locations often costing more. This makes them a more hands-on form of building income when compared to selling to restaurants or grocery stores, but they can be a profitable endeavor if you can afford the time. One of the terrific advantages that the farmer market has is it allows you to talk to your customers face-to-face. You can let them know when you'll be back or where they can find more. Adding a face to a brand makes people much more likely to buy your product next time they're debating between it and another. They've met you before, so they can feel good by supporting you. That same purchase they were planning to make anyway is swung in your favor in a manner that leaves the customer feeling satisfied. A little bit of the hands-on selling with a friendly smile, and you can earn yourself some loyal customers.

Roadside Attractions

Roadside attractions are often used to sell produce and other vegetables. This can be achieved without having to spend your time watching over the setup. A box for payment can be locked into place, and payment then proceeds on the honor system. This works for vegetables because they love the light. Mushrooms, not quite so much. That factor can make a roadside attraction less appealing as a way of earning money.

But, if you can create some shade in the design, then you can get away with this approach. Some species will have no problems, others will be iffy, and some are going to be best handled and sold in a different way.

These are also gourmet mushrooms, so the demand for them at a roadside booth is going to be much smaller. On the other hand, if you are selling lots of varieties of mushrooms, then you may want to convert a shed or garage into a mini-attraction. You can offer shade and environmental stability for the mushrooms while also creating an experience for the customers. You can offer more products this way and more species. Admittedly, this can be an expensive approach to set up, but it can become an absolutely incredible money-making approach with some marketing and word of mouth.

Dried Mushrooms and Alternative Products

Chapter Seven discussed the way that we can preserve our mushrooms by drying them or turning them into sauces. Both of these can make a decent profit, as long as you know who your target customers are. Dried mushrooms aren't going to be a hot product at a farmers' market. But chefs and restaurants love purchasing them to add some flavor and texture to their soups. Chefs will be interested in these dried mushrooms, but they aren't going to want to purchase your mushroom sauces. They are far more likely to make their own house blend for use across several dishes they offer. Still, sauces and pickled mushrooms or healthy snacks such as a blend of dried mushrooms and peas, all of these sell well at farmers' markets, and some grocery stores will consider stocking local sauces and treats.

Dried mushrooms and alternative products give you ways of offering variety in your products throughout the year. Always sell your mushrooms when they are fresh, but don't get too anxious if they don't all sell. There are plenty of ways to diversify your wares and reduce waste.

MUSHROOM CULTIVATION

Chapter Summary

- As discussed in the first chapter, one of the best places to sell your mushrooms is to local restaurants that need fresh mushrooms for their dishes. Call the restaurant before you start your mushroom cultivation to see what kinds they serve and use already.

- Grocery stores are useful customers because they will buy in large quantities if the quality is good. But grocery stores need to see that there is a demand for the product. When cultivating gourmet mushrooms, it is best to approach high-end or gourmet stores that cater to the type of clientele that's willing to pay more for gourmet products.

- Farmers' markets require you to rent a table and spend time physically maintaining and looking after it. This makes it a time-consuming approach to selling, but it gets you face-to-face with customers, and this helps you to create brand loyalty.

- A roadside attraction such as a small barn converted into a mushroom store can earn lots of money in the long run. It requires more time and effort to set up and to market, but you can cut out the middleman and sell your mushrooms directly to the consumer this way. Small communities often love roadside attractions of a wholesome nature such as this, and they become pleasant social experiences for the customer.

- Dried mushrooms can be sold to restaurants and chefs to add to soups and stews. Mushroom mixtures such as pickled mushrooms or mushroom sauces can be sold at stores or farmers' markets. Both of these take mushrooms that would have gone bad in a few days and extend their lifespan by upwards of a year.

In the next chapter, you will learn some amazing and delicious recipes that will make your mushrooms taste better than you could even believe.

CHAPTER 10

DELICIOUS RECIPES FOR MUSHROOM LOVERS

Throughout this book, I've continued to mention how delicious mushrooms are. It's only fair that I share a couple of recipes with you so you can find out for yourself. Mushrooms can be sliced or diced to accentuate pizza, pasta, and stir-fries. The two recipes we look at will emphasize the mushroom itself. From a quick snack or healthy side dish to a creamy soup, these dishes offer just a glimpse at the flavor possibilities mushrooms offer.

MUSHROOM CULTIVATION

Garlic Mushrooms

Garlic mushrooms are our snack or side dish, depending on your tastes. They're so savory that they make a filling, healthy snack with very little effort. Don't even get me started on how good they taste draped over a fresh steak. You're going to need a few spices and a bit of butter. When first making garlic mushrooms, stick to mushrooms of the same type and roughly the same size. It'll be easier to cook them to be ready at the same time. But this recipe is so simple, you can use it with different mushrooms or mix several kinds together. Just be mindful of the fact that they will cook at different rates.

Break out the frying pan and toss on a lot of butter. This is one of those cases where more is an advantage. The more butter you use, the more they will be dripping with garlic sauce goodness when you spoon them onto a plate. You will want to spice them to taste, but for the best garlic mushrooms, you need to use garlic, then a little bit of salt and pepper. A dash of thyme will really make the whole flavor pop in your mouth.

So, for a pound of mushrooms, use four tablespoons of butter (or more). One tablespoon of garlic powder. Salt and pepper and other herbs to taste.

The butter is melted in the frying pan. Use a medium heat, and make sure to spread the butter throughout the pan. The mushrooms are tossed in, along with salt and pepper and any other herbs you are using. On a medium heat, it should take about seven minutes for your mushrooms to begin to change color and saute. Add the garlic, then cook for half a minute to let the flavors combine. Remove from heat and serve!

Creamy Mushroom Soup

The creamy mushroom soup is more involved than the garlic mushrooms, but that doesn't mean it is less delicious. For this you will need:

MUSHROOM CULTIVATION

- A quarter cup of butter.

- Bit of salt.

- A diced onion.

- 1 cup of heavy whipping cream.

- 1 cup of water.

- 4 cups of chicken broth.

- 2 pounds of mushrooms, sliced.

- A tablespoon and a half of flour.

- 2 peeled cloves of garlic.

It'll take about an hour and a half to cook, so keep that in mind when you schedule this one.

Begin by melting your butter in your soup pot. You'll cook your mushrooms in this butter, keeping an eye to watch for when they start to release their juice. When you notice they are, drop the temperature down to low. You want the juices to evaporate slowly. The mushrooms will be turning a darker brown color, and everything should be ready in fifteen minutes or so. If you like, this is a good point to remove a couple of mushrooms to put on top of the soup when served. If you are ready to continue, then you add your onion into the mixture and take another few minutes for the onion to soften.

When the onion is ready, add your flour and cook it for two minutes. Stir once every fifteen seconds. After the flour has been stirring into the mixture, add the garlic, the chicken broth, and the water together. Stir it together so that everything is mixed. Keep it on a low heat and cover the pot with a lid. Set a timer for an hour and let it cook. Remove the pot from the heat when the timer goes off. The soup is moved over to a blender and pureed. Stir in heavy whipping cream after all the soup has been blended.

You now have yourself a delicious and creamy mushroom soup that will knock your socks off. Add salt and pepper, some thyme, or a few sauteed mushrooms to accentuate the flavor, and really create a gorgeous display.

FINAL WORDS

We've covered a lot of ground in this book and learned everything that beginners need to know when it comes to cultivating mushrooms. To close up, let's take a quick look at what we covered and where to go from here.

We began this book by looking at the benefits of cultivating our own mushrooms. From providing food to improving the soil and increasing our fortunes, there are many reasons that make mushroom farming so appealing. Chapter Two gave a brief overview of the mushroom farming process. We saw how we start our mushrooms in the lab, create a spawn, and then grow the mushrooms themselves. This set up much of what we would be looking at in more detail later in the book.

Chapter Three was a deep dive into the different kinds of gourmet mushrooms you may want to grow yourself. I have recommended that you start with oyster mushrooms, and I stick by that. For beginners, they offer enough challenge and enough control to make it a fun learning experience.

In Chapter Four, we looked at how we can create a grow room and a lab, two parts of the mushroom farm. You don't need either when starting out, but they are great steps for future expansion. A grow room can focus on one method of growing, or it can support multiple methods. We used Chapter Five to explore these different approaches. You will want to match the approach to the species you are growing, not try to force a species to grow in a particular method if it isn't what it requires. Chapter Six saw us put together everything we learned and create a simple and easy mushroom crop for beginners using cardboard, bags, and oyster mushrooms.

In Chapter Seven, we saw how to preserve our mushrooms. If we can't sell or cook them all, then we're going to want to freeze, dry, or pickle them. This ties Chapter Seven in closely with Chapter Nine, where we looked at how we can profit by selling mushrooms to grocery stores or at farmers' markets. Chapter Eight looked at fungi to show that while every mushroom is a fungus, not every fungus is a mushroom. We also took a quick look at just how beneficial the various forms of fungus are to the world. We closed out on Chapter Ten, and a couple of tasty recipes I can't wait for you to try.

Where you go from here is up to you. The information necessary to expand from a single bag of oyster mushrooms to a full mushroom growing operation is in your hands. You need to implement that information and act on it, but you have what it takes to get started. Begin slow, but don't be afraid to work your way up and start growing bigger and bigger batches of gourmet mushrooms. They can make you a lot of money. I certainly hope that they bring you lots. But the money doesn't flow without the mushrooms, so go clean your hands, and start growing your first batch today.

www.ingramcontent.com/pod-product-compliance
Lightning Source LLC
Chambersburg PA
CBHW050313120526
44592CB00014B/1886